Understanding Your
Potential

by Myles Munroe

Destiny Image Publishers
P.O. Box 351
Shippensburg, PA 17257-0351

"Speaking to the Purposes of God for this Generation"

ISBN # 1-56043-046-X

For Worldwide Distribution
Printed in the U.S.A.

Contents

Dedication
Acknowledgments
Foreword
Preface
Introduction

Dedication

To my daughter and son, Charisa and Chairo (Myles Jr.), may your potential be maximized in your generation.

To my parents, Matt and Louise, and all my ten brothers and sisters for your encouragement and support.

And to all the "Third World" peoples throughout the world for whom I live and breathe that you may come to know Jesus Christ, the only One who can truly help you to understand and realize your true and full *potential*.

Acknowledgments

We are a sum total of what we have learned from all who have taught us, both great and small. I am grateful for the inspiration and wisdom of the men and women of God and for the transgenerational sources and roots of wisdom they left me.

I am also grateful for the many members, friends and colleagues at Bahamas Faith Ministries International whose faithfulness, prayers and patience inspire me to continue to fulfill my purpose and potential.

For the development and production of the book itself, I feel a deep sense of gratitude to:

—my precious wife, Ruth, and our children, Charisa and Chairo (Myles Jr.), for their patience and support during my travels outside the home. You make it easier to fulfill God's will for my life.

—my father and mother, Matt and Louise Munroe, for their devotion to the Lord and their children, and their constant demonstration of love that inspired me to pursue the maximization of my potential.

—my dear friend and brother-in-law whose commitment to the work and vision make this project possible.

—Kathy Miller, my gifted and diligent transcriber, editor and advisor, who shepherded the book from its early formless stage to its present form, and Marsha Peck, of Destiny Image, who patiently pursued me to keep to the schedule and meet the deadlines.

—the best friends in the ministry I can ever have—Ternel Nelson, Bertril Baird, Peter Morgan, John Smith, Kingsley Fletcher, Fuschia Pickett, Ezekiel Guti and Jerry Horner—for exposing my potential.

Foreword

Years ago I read a brief biography that summarizes the life span of myriad of people who are harnessed to the treadmill of the trivial, never having responded to the challenge to leave the commonplace of mediocrity and ascend to the higher dimension of fulfilled potentialities. Perhaps you remember this celebrated biography:

Solomon Grunday...Born on Monday...
Christened on Tuesday...Married on Wednesday...
Taken ill on Thursday...Worse on Friday...
Died on Saturday...Buried on Sunday...
And that was the end of Solomon Grunday.

Perhaps a bland life story like this is encouraged by an apathetic society that prefers the easy shortcut to the hard productive way, exalts goofing off rather than diligence, promotes a work ethic that concentrates more on what is due me than on what I owe, shrugs its shoulders rather than extend a helping hand, replies to every call to action with "what's in it for me?" and prefers to sit out a problem rather than sweat out a solution. That nonchalant and perfunctory attitude is a powerful tool of satan in his efforts to retard the growth of God's Kingdom. Many unwary Christians have been subjugated by his beguiling appeal to "take life easy."

People generally fall into one of three groups: the few who make things happen, the many who watch things happen and the overwhelming majority who have no notion of what happens. Every person is either a creator of fact or a creature of circumstance. He either puts color into his environment, or, like a chameleon, takes color from his environment. Or to put it another way: Some people are thermometers. They conform completely to their environment—their behavior is definitely determined from without. Other people are thermostats. Instead of allowing their environment to control them, they determine the environment.

In this book, Myles Munroe dares us to leave the beaten path of mediocrity and blaze adventurous new trails that will tax us to the limit of our abilities and squeeze from us every contribution we could possibly make for the glory of God and the good of society. It's an exacting challenge, but living up to it will cause us to leave footprints that are both deep enough for others to follow and correctly aligned so as to lead in the right direction.

No one who reads this book with an open heart and mind will ever again prefer the common, settle for less than the best or stop short of the extremity of his capabilities. The person who accepts the challenge presented herein won't pick up the bench when there is a piano to be moved, sit in a corner when there is a continent to traverse or splash in the wading pool when there is an ocean to cross. In Shakespeare's *Othello*, Iago said of Desdemona, "She counts it a vice in her virtue not to do more than she is asked to do." This book calls upon us to possess the same outlook.

Everyone who reads this volume must come to the conclusion that success is not a comparison of what we have done with what others have done. It is simply coming up to the level of our best, making the most of our abilities and possibilities. Myles Munroe is a living example of the type person he calls us to be. He is one of those rare individuals who lives life to the maximum. Splendidly gifted by God with extraordinary talents in areas that most of us only wish about—music, art, preaching, teaching, administration, diplomacy, writing and even spear fishing—he refuses to allow any of God's gifts to stagnate. It would be easy to envy this man or to blame God for shortchanging me when He dispensed gifts. But according to Ephesians 2:10, I am God's poem (the literal meaning of "workmanship"), enabled by Him to walk along the course He has ordained especially for me. Just as Peter was accountable for himself and not John (John 21:20-22), I must accept responsibility for myself and not Myles. It's comforting to know that whenever God gives me a task, He places at my disposal all the resources of heaven. I am not left to my own devices to accomplish that task. Canon Farrar stated it in these words:

I am only one.	What I can do
But I am one.	I ought to do.
I cannot do everything,	And what I ought to do
But I can do something.	By the grace of God I will do.

Jerry Horner
Virginia Beach, Virginia
May 9, 1991

Preface

The wealthiest spot on this planet is not the oil fields of Kuwait, Iraq or Saudi Arabia. Neither is it the gold and diamond mines of South Africa, the uranium mines of the Soviet Union or the silver mines of Africa. Though it may surprise you, the richest deposits on our planet lie just a few blocks from your house. They rest in your local cemetery or graveyard. Buried beneath the soil within the walls of those sacred grounds are dreams that never came to pass, songs that were never sung, books that were never written, paintings that never filled a canvas, ideas that were never shared, visions that never became reality, inventions that were never designed, plans that never went beyond the drawing board of the mind and purposes that were never fulfilled. Our graveyards are filled with potential that remained potential. *What a tragedy!*

As I walk the streets of our cities, my heart frequently weeps as I encounter and observe the wasted, broken, disoriented lives of individuals who, years before, were talented, intelligent, aspiring high-school classmates. During their youth they had dreams, desires, plans and aspirations. Today they are lost in a maze of substance abuse, alcoholism, purposelessness and poorly chosen friends. Their lives are aimless, their decisions haphazard. This enormous tragedy saddens me. *What* could *have been* has become *what should have been.* The *wealth of dreams* has been dashed into the *poverty of discouragement.*

Only a minute percentage of the five billion people on this planet will experience a significant portion of their true potential. Are you a candidate for contributing to the wealth of the cemetery? Ask yourself the following questions.

Who am I?

Why am I here?

How much potential do I have?

What am I capable of doing?

By what criteria should I measure my ability?

Who sets the standards?

By what process can I maximize my ability?

What are my limitations?

Within the answers to these questions lies the key to a fulfilled, effective life.

One of the greatest tragedies in life is to watch potential die untapped. Many potentially great men and women never realize their potential because they do not understand the nature and concept of the potential principle. As God has revealed to me the nature of potential, I have received a burden to teach others what I have learned.

There's a wealth of potential in you. I know, because God has shown me the vast store He placed in me. My purpose is to help you understand that potential and get it out. *You* must decide if you are going to rob the world or bless it with the rich, valuable, potent, untapped resources locked away within you.

You are more than what you have done.

Introduction

The brilliant summer sun poured its liquid heat on the windswept island of the Caribbean paradise as the old village sculptor made his way to his humble home outside the village center. On his way he passed by the great white mansion of the plantation owner who, with his field workers, was felling one of the age-old trees that for generations had provided protection from the scorching sun. The old sculptor suddenly stopped and, with a twinkle in his eyes, called over the wall with a note of interest, "What will you do with those discarded stumps of wood?"

The owner replied, "These are good for nothing but firewood. I have no used for this junk."

The old sculptor begged for a piece of the "junk" wood and with care lifted the knotted tree trunk to his shoulders. With a smile of gratitude, he staggered into the distance carrying his burdensome treasure.

After entering his cottage, the old man placed the jagged piece of tree in the center of the floor. Then, in a seemingly mysterious and ceremonious manner, he walked around what the plantation owner had called "useless junk." As the old man picked up his hammer and chisel, a strange smile pierced his leathered face. Attacking the wood, he worked as though under a mandate to set something free from the gnarled, weathered trunk.

The following morning, the sun found the sculptor asleep on the floor of his cottage, clutching a beautifully sculptured bird. He had freed the bird from the bondage of the junk wood. Later he placed the bird on the railing of his front porch and forgot it.

Weeks later the plantation owner came by to visit. When he saw the bird, he asked to buy it—offering whatever price the sculptor might name. Satisfied that he had made an excellent bargain, the gentleman walked away, hugging to his breast with great pride the newly acquired treasure. The old sculptor, sitting on the steps of his simple cottage, counted his spoil and thought, "Junk is in the eyes of the beholder. Some look, but others see."

Today there are many individuals whose lives are like the old tree. Trapped within them is a beautiful bird of potential that may never fly. Society, like the plantation owner, sees nothing in them but a useless, worthless person on his way to the garbage heap of life. But we must remember that one man's junk is another man's jewel.

Scientists in the field of human potential have estimated that we use as little as ten percent of our abilities. Ninety percent of our capabilities lie dormant and wasted. It is sad that we use only a small part of our abilities and talents. Most of us have no idea how much talent and potential we possess.

Consider the life of Abraham Lincoln. His story is one of the most dramatic examples of a man struggling to release the wealth of potential locked up inside him:

He lost his job in 1832.
He was elected to the legislature in 1834.
He suffered the death of his sweetheart in 1834.
He suffered a nervous breakdown in 1836.
He was defeated for speaker of the State Legislature in 1838.
He was defeated for nomination for Congress in 1843.
He was elected to Congress in 1846.
He was rejected for the position of land officer in 1849.
He was defeated for the Senate in 1854.
He was defeated for the nomination for vice-president of the United States in 1856.
He again was defeated for the Senate in 1858.
He was elected president of the United States in 1869.

Everything in life was created with potential and possesses the potential principle. In every seed there is a tree...in every bird a flock...in every fish a school...in every sheep a flock...in every cow a herd...in every boy a man...in every girl a woman...in every nation a generation. Tragedy strikes when a tree dies in a seed, a man in a boy, a woman in a girl, an idea in a mind. For untold millions, visions die unseen, songs die unsung, plans die unexecuted and futures die buried in the past. The problems of our world go unanswered because potential remains buried.

The Bible tells a story about talents and potential. The talents in the story are symbols of the vast store of abilities our Creator has planted within us. In the story, the master of the estate entrusts some of his wealth to three of his servants. The first man invests his talent and doubles the wealth the master had entrusted to his care. The second servant also doubles what the master had given him. With them the master is very pleased. Finally the master turns to the third servant and asks, "What have you done with your talent?"

The servant answered, "I was afraid to misuse the talent, so I carefully hid it. Here it is. I am giving it back to you in the same condition that I received it."

In fury the master rebuked his servant, "You wicked and lazy servant. How dare you not use the gifts I gave to you?" "Take my money from him and throw this useless fellow into the street."

We are responsible for the potential stored within us. We must learn to understand it and effectively use it. Too often our successes prevent us from seeking that which yet lies within us. Success becomes our enemy as we settle for what we have. Refuse to be satisfied with your last accomplishment, because potential never has a retirement plan. Do not let what you *cannot* do interfere with what you *can* do. In essence, what you see is not all there is.

1 Everything in Life Has Potential

All men are sent to the world with limitless credit, but seldom draw to their full extent.

It is a tragedy to know that with over five billion people on this planet today, only a minute percentage will experience a significant fraction of their true potential. Perhaps you are a candidate for contributing to the wealth of the cemetery. Your potential was not given for you to deposit in the grave. You must understand the tremendous potential you possess and commit yourself to maximizing it in your short lifetime. What is potential, anyway?

Potential Defined

Potential is...dormant ability...reserved power...untapped strength...unused success...hidden talents...capped capability.

All you can be but have not yet become...all you can do but have not yet done...how far you can reach but have not yet reached...what you can accomplish but have not yet accomplished. Potential is unexposed ability and latent power.

Potential is therefore not what you have done, but what you are yet able to do. In other words, what you have done is no longer your potential. What you have successfully accomplished is no longer potential. It is said that unless you do something beyond what you have done, you will never grow or experience your full potential. Potential demands that you never settle for what you have accomplished. One of the great enemies of your potential is success. In order to realize your full potential, you must never be satisfied with your last accomplishment. It is also important that you never let what you *cannot do* interfere with what you *can do.* The greatest tragedy in life is not death, but a life that never realized its full potential. You must decide today not to rob the world of the rich, valuable, potent, untapped resources locked away within you. *Potential never has a retirement plan.*

The Potential Principle

To simplify this concept let us look at one of the most powerful elements in nature...the seed. If I held a seed in my hand and asked you, "What do I have in my hand?" what would you say? Perhaps you would answer what seems to be the obvious...a seed. However, if you understand the nature of a seed, your answer would be *fact* but not *truth.*

The truth is I hold a forest in my hand. Why? Because in every seed there is a tree, and in every tree there are fruit or flowers with seeds in them. And these seeds also have trees that have fruit that have seeds...that have trees that have fruit that have seeds, etc. In essence, *what you see is not all there is. That is potential. Not what is, but what could be.*

God created everything with potential, including you. He placed the seed of each thing within itself (Genesis 1:12), and planted within each person or thing He created the ability to be much more than it is at any one moment. Thus, everything in life has potential.

Nothing Is Instant

Nothing in life is instant. People think miracles are instant, but they really are not. They are just a process that has been sped up. Nothing God created is instant, because God does not operate in the instant. He is a God of the potential principle. Everything begins as potential.

He did not create a ready-made human race—the earth was not given an instant population. God made one person—not a million people. He started with one seed. Then from that one He created another. Then he said to those seeds, "Bless you (that means, 'You have My permission'). Be fruitful and multiply and replenish the earth."

In Adam, God gave the earth a seed with the potential of one...one hundred...one thousand...one million... The five billion people on the earth today were in that one man's loins. God knew that in Adam and Eve there were enough people to fill the earth. That's the way God works. He knows the potential principle because He introduced it. It is Him.

Don't Settle for What You Have

Potential is always present, waiting to be exposed. It demands that you never settle for what you have accomplished. One of the greatest enemies of your potential is success. God wants you to maximize the potential He has given to you. You are not yet what you are supposed to be—though you may be pleased with what you now are. Don't accept your present state in life as final, because it is just that, a state. Don't be satisfied with your last accomplishment, because there are many accomplishments yet to be perfected. Since you are full of potential, you should not be the same person next year that you are this year.

Never accept success as a lifestyle—it is but a phase. Never accept an accomplishment as the end—it is but a mark in the process. Because you are God's offspring, there are many selves within you that lie dormant, untapped and unused. Your primary problem is that you do not think like God does.

**There are many selves within you
that lie dormant, untapped and unused.**

God is always looking for what is not yet visible. He expects to find inside each person and thing He created more than is evident on the outside. On the other hand, man is often satisfied with what he has—or at least if not satisfied, he thinks there is nothing better. Thus he settles for what he has.

Therein lies the tragedy of life. The minute we begin to settle down and be satisfied with what we have, we lose the possibility of revealing what is really inside us. Too often we die without exploring the gifts, abilities and successes that lay hidden within us. Our thoughts, ideas and possibilities are not used. We fail to realize the vast potential that is stored within us. We are like batteries in a radio that is never played—our potential is wasted.

Suppose...

Suppose Shakespeare had died before he wrote his poems and plays—the potential of Macbeth would have been buried. Suppose Michelangelo had died before he painted the Cistene Chapel or Rembrandt the Mona Lisa—the beauty of their paintings would have been lost. Suppose Mozart had died with all that music in his bosom.

Suppose Moses had died before he saw the burning bush...Paul before he met Jesus on the Damascus Road... Abraham before Isaac was born. How different the pages of Scripture and history would be. Suppose Martin Luther had died without writing the theses...Charles Wesley without penning the hymns...John Wycliff without translating the Bible into English. How different the history of the Church might have been.

Can you imagine how many great works of art, music and literature are buried in the graveyard near your house? Can you imagine how many solutions to the problems we face today are buried with someone you knew? People die without getting out their full potential. They fail to use all that was stored in them for the benefit of the world.

Don't Die With My Things!

I wonder what would have happened if your father had died before you were conceived or your mother before you were born. What would the world have lost if you had not been born? What will the world lack because you fail to live out your potential? Will you carry songs, books, inventions, cures or discoveries to your grave?

What would the world have lost if you had not been born?

Our teens are committing suicide. I wonder who they were supposed to be and what they were supposed to do that we will never know. Have we lost some great leaders? Was your grandchild's professor or another Martin Luther King among them?

As the time for His crucifixion drew near, Jesus spoke of the potential principle in terms of His life. He compared Himself to a kernel of wheat that falls into the ground and dies (John 12:23-24). A kernel of wheat, when planted, yields many more kernels. Within Jesus was the potential to bring millions of people to God. Thank God Herod didn't succeed when he tried to wipe out Jesus. If he had, Jesus would have died before He could offer Himself as our atonement. His great purpose in life would have been wasted. The seed of His life was much more than His disciples could see. That one seed had the potential to give life to many.

There was a time early in his ministry when the apostle Paul said, "I'd like to leave." Though he preferred to die and be with Christ, he knew his purpose in life had not been completely fulfilled. There was yet much fruitful labor for him to do. It was necessary for the Church that he continue to live. Thank God Paul did not die. The benefit of his wisdom would have been lost to the early Church and to us. His potential to write Colossians and Ephesians may have been forfeited.

Later, near his death, Paul wrote: "Timothy, I've run the race. I've finished the course. I've kept the faith. I've done the work. My award awaits me. I'm ready to die. Keep working after I'm gone" (2 Timothy 4:5-7). Everything in life has the potential to fulfill its purpose. *People who die without achieving their full potential rob their generation of their latent ability.* Many have robbed me—they've also robbed you. *To die with ability is irresponsible.*

Perhaps you are wasting your life doing nothing with all you have. God packaged some things in you for the good of the world—use it. We will never know the wealth God planted in you until you bring it up. There's always something in you that we haven't yet seen because that's the way God thinks. Release your ability before you die. Use the power and strength within you for the good of yourself and others. I believe there are books, songs, art works, businesses, poems, inventions and investments in you that God intended for my children to enjoy. Don't give up until you have lived out the full extent of your potential, because *you have no right to die with my things.* Don't rob the next generation of the wealth, treasure and tremendous gifts buried deep within you.

If you want to succeed, strike out on new paths. Don't travel the worn paths of accepted success.

No man can climb beyond the limitations of his own belief.

Every day sends to the grave obscure men and women whom fear prevented from realizing their true and full potential.

Failure is not the absence of success. Failure is the neglect of trying.

What you see is not all there is. There is something in everything.

PRINCIPLE: What you have done is no longer your potential. Potential is what you can do but have not yet done.

PRINCIPLES

---

1. God created everything with potential.

2. Nothing in life is instant.

3. Everything in life has the potential to fulfill its purpose.

4. Don't be satisfied with what you now are.

5. Don't die without using your full potential.

6. The greatest threat to progress is your last successful accomplishment.

2 The Source of All Potential

The potential of a thing is related to its source.

Everything in life was created with potential and possesses the potential principle. Creation abounds with potential because the Creator Himself *is* the potential principle.

When we describe God, we often say He is omnipotent. *Omnipotent* means that *God is always potent*. Made up of two words: *omni*, meaning "always," and *potent*, meaning "full of power," *omnipotent* means that God is potentially everything. He has within Him the potential for all that is, was or ever will be. He is omni-potent or omnipotent.

Everything Comes From God

Everything that was and everything that is was in God. That's a very important concept. Everything that was and is, was in God. We have to start with God. Before God made anything, before He created things, there was only God. So before anything was, God is. God is the root, or source, of all life.

Before anything was, God is.

Before there was time, time was—but it was in God. Before God created a galaxy or the Milky Way, they existed. Before there was a universe or a planetary system with the fourth planet called earth revolving around the sun—before any of that was—they were.

I wonder what it must have been like when God was just by Himself. Let's try to imagine that for a bit. Here's God. He steps out on nothing to view nothing, for there was nothing except God. And so God is standing on top of nothing, looking at nothing because everything was in Him.

In God Was the Beginning

The Bible tells us: "In the beginning, God..." That means before there was a beginning, there was God. Therefore, God began the beginning and verse 0 of the first chapter of Genesis might possibly read: In God was the beginning. Everything that is was in God. Everything that has ever been made was made by God.

When we connect Genesis 1:0—in God was the beginning—and John 1:1—in the beginning was the Word, and the Word was with God...He was with God in the beginning—we see that the Word was with God *in* the beginning, not *at* the beginning.

Before there was a beginning,
there was God.
Everything that is was in God.

The Gospel of John also tells us that all things were made by the Word.

In the beginning was the Word, and the Word was with God, and the Word was God. He was with God in the beginning. Through Him all things were made; without

Him nothing was made that has been made. In Him was life... (John 1:1-4)

Nothing that was created was made without the Word. In *the Word* was life. *Life* came out of God. Therefore, before you knew life, life was. *All* things were made by God. Everything you see, hear, smell, taste and touch was in God before they came to be. Even what you discern first existed in God.

Now let me be a little ridiculous to prove my point. God had roaches and mosquitoes and rats in Him. He had suns and clouds and planets in Him. The cows to make shoe leather...the oil to run our cars...the ore from the mountains to make steel—all these things were in God. Everything on this earth is God's property. If God would ever call in His property, we would be in big trouble. All things were in God and thus belong to Him. God, in the beginning when there was nothing, contained everything that man *has seen.* He also contained everything man *will ever see.*

Thus if you had talked to God on the highway of nothingness, you would have been talking to millions of cows and horses and mountains and trees and limousines and hotels and beaches. They all were in God. They were in Him, but no one saw them. That's why we call God omnipotent. He's always full of the potential to bring forth what you see. God is pregnant with the universe. In essence, if you met God on the highway of nothing, by the corner of nowhere, before there was anything, and you shook His hand, you would be shaking hands with *everything*, but would not know it. You would *be* with potential.

The Invisible Became Visible

In the beginning, God was pregnant with the universe and all things were made by Him. But how did these things come out of Him? How was the universe formed? All things were formed at God's command. He spat them out—poof!

From the invisible came the visible. Things that are seen came from things that were unseen.

> **By faith we understand that the universe was formed at God's command, so that what is seen was not made out of what was visible** (Hebrews 11:3).

God always had everything in Him, but we couldn't see it. All we now see was once in an invisible state. Everything that man has ever seen first existed in an invisible state. (Please note that invisible does not mean nonexistent.)

All the buildings we see and the businesses we frequent—people making money and investing money—all that stuff began as ideas. We couldn't see them because they were in somebody's mind. The stores where we shop, also everything on the shelves and racks in those stores, began as ideas in someone's mind. They didn't exist before, yet they did. Although they weren't present in their current form, they existed as lumber and concrete and nails, cotton and wool and flax, steel and pulleys and motors.

Someone had an idea. Through work they put their idea into things that are visible. Today they take your money. Everything starts in the invisible state. Everything we now see used to be unseen.

In the beginning there was only God. At creation the entire unseen universe became visible. Everything that has been created was made by the word of God. Although it already existed, God spoke so that what was invisible could become visible. You would never have known it existed, except God spat it out in faith.

By faith God spat out what was in Him. Everything in Him started to come forth. What we now see was birthed by God from what was invisibly within Him. Whatever you see came from the unseen—nothing exists that was not at some time in God. Thus, *faith is not the evidence of things that do not exist. It is the evidence of things that are not yet seen.* Everything we see has always been. It became visible when God *spoke* it into being. God is the source of life.

Spoke Was Hard Work

What happened when God spoke at creation? How did He get the invisible to become visible? First let me broaden your idea of the word *spoke*.

Spoke was a process. What God spoke into visibility began as an idea in His mind. God first conceived in His mind what He wanted to create. He didn't just say, "I want this." The prophet Isaiah tells us that God created the earth by first planning its foundations (Isaiah 48:13). After the plans were in His mind, God spoke them into existence. When God was ready to speak, it was just a matter of taking what was in the plan and putting it on the site.

Spoke was a process.

God laid the groundwork for the earth and spread out the heavens. He created the sun to shine during the day and the moon and stars at night. He gave every star a name. He ordered clouds to fill the sky and breezes to blow. He made the waves to roar in the sea. He sent rain to water the earth and grass to cover the hillside. Thunder and lightening were created by His command; hail and sleet were formed by His word. A wool-like blanket of snow He produced for winter; frost and dew He designed.

God was full of imagination. He was pregnant with many thoughts. His thoughts became ideas, and the ideas became images. Everything that is came out of God as He *spoke* those images. The unseen became seen—the invisible became visible.

God's speaking was much like the contractions of a woman in labor. With effort He pushed out each detailed creation. Then God began organizing the things that appeared. He was busy as He set them up, organizing and organizing and reorganizing. Finally God said, "This is good."

God didn't create the world by just *thinking* the whole thing into being. He *worked* it into being. After creating a plan in His mind, God spoke to make visible the invisible. (Speaking was one of the ways He worked.) All that was made came from God. Through work He created the world.

For six days God created the heavens and the earth. On the seventh day He rested.

By the seventh day God had finished the work He had been doing; so on the seventh day He rested from all His work. And God blessed the seventh day and made it holy, because on it He rested from all the work of creating that He had done (Genesis 2:2-3).

Spoke must be a fairly serious thing. If God, who is almighty and all powerful, had to rest after creation, *spoke it* must have been very hard work.

When creation was completed, God rested. God was the first one to *sabbat*—He intended the Sabbath to be a blessing. He knows that life produces work, and work creates the need to rest.

The Work of Creation Is Not Yet Complete

The work of God is not complete—He has not delivered all His babies. He will keep on delivering as long as you deliver, because *you* are the continuation of His deliveries. God can still create. When you ask for something in prayer, God doesn't have to shift things around because He is going broke. If it doesn't exist in a visible form, God will speak it.

He'll make whatever is necessary. He continues to be pregnant with many things.

Because all things are in God, you can ask God for anything. An idea is around in God a long time before it comes out. Nothing we think or do is new (Ecclesiastes 1:9). Everything that has been done will be done again—what we think is new has already been here for a long time.

Nothing we think or do is new.

There's a guy in China right now who is thinking about the idea you thought was yours. When the idea came out of God, many people got it. Because everything comes out of God, you all received the idea from the same Source. Until that idea is transformed by action, God will continue to leak that idea into men and women. Why? Because God is a God of potential. Although *He* is the source of all things, He shares His omnipotent powers with His creation. We, like God, are pregnant with many things. We are full of imagination, having the potential power to be more than we visibly are. There are dreams, visions, plans and ideas in us that need to be released. God wants us to tap His power and use it, because God made us with potential.

PRINCIPLES

1. Everything that was and is, was in God.

2. God is the Source of all potential.

3. All things were formed at God's command so the invisible became visible.

4. God planned the world in His mind before speaking it into existence.

3 | Who Are You?

Who you are is related to where you came from.

Many Look, Few See

A sculptor works in a very interesting way. I'm an artist of sorts, so I have a bit of an understanding how artists work. One thing I have learned is that you never argue with an artist until he is finished. Don't discuss anything with a painter or a sculptor until his work is completed. An artist can be very rude if you disturb him before he has accomplished what he intends to do, because he sees differently than those who are not artists.

An artist can walk by the stone in your front yard and see a figure in it. He may stop by your house and beg you for a stone you have walked past many times without noticing. The dogs may have been doing stuff on it. You may even have been planning to get rid of it because it's a nuisance. But the artist walks into your yard and sees something beautiful in that stone beyond what you can imagine.

Two months later when the artist invites you to his workshop he says, "Do you see that? Do you know where that came from?"

"England or France?" you ask.

"No," says the artist. "It came from your yard."

"Do you mean...?"

"Yes."

"Five hundred dollars, please."

You were sitting on five hundred dollars. The dogs were doing stuff on five hundred dollars. But you couldn't see the potential in the rock.

You Are Not Junk

There are many people who are being passed by because others don't see what is in them. But God has shown me what's in me, and I know it is in you too. My job is to stop you and say: "Can you see what's in you? Do you know your potential? Do you know that you are not just someone born in a ghetto over the hill? There's a wealth of potential in you."

A sculptor sees so differently. They say Michelangelo used to walk around a block of marble for days—just walking around it, talking to himself. First he would see things in the rock; then he would go and take them out.

Insight like that of a sculptor is seen in the Bible. When the world dumps and rejects you, and you land on the garbage heap of the world, God walks along and picks you up. He looks deep within you and sees a person of great worth.

Don't ever let anybody throw you away. You are not junk. When God looks at you, He sees things that everybody else ignores. You are worth so much that Jesus went to Calvary to salvage and reclaim you. The Spirit of God connected to your spirit is the only true judge of your worth. Don't accept the opinions of others because they do not see what God sees.

When God looks at you, He sees things that everybody else ignores.

God Looked and Saw...

God looked at Adam and saw a world. He looked at Abraham and saw nations. In Jacob, a deceiver, He saw a Messiah. In Moses the murderer, God saw a deliverer. Can you imagine looking at a stammering young man and seeing the greatest leader in history?

God saw a king in a shepherd boy. When the Israelites wanted a king, God sent Samuel to the home of Jesse. When Jesse heard why Samuel was there, he dressed up all his sons—the handsome one, the tall one, the curly-haired one, the strong one, the muscular one. All the sons of Jesse twirled out before Samuel, from the greatest to the least. With his vase of anointing oil, Samuel watched Jesse's show as he presented his sons: "This is my intelligent son who graduated from the University of I Don't Know What." After the guy gave a speech, Samuel said, "No." The next son came out dressed like Pat Paulson and God said, "No." A third son gave a nice speech about philosophy and again God said, "No." Finally, after Jesse had paraded all of his sons before him, Samuel said, "I'm sorry. None of these is God's choice for king. Do you have any other sons?"

Then Jesse said, "Yes...well no. I just remembered. I do have a little boy, my youngest son. He's just a little runt who's out taking care of the sheep. He's not dressed up like my other sons, nor have his hands been manicured and his body scented with perfumes from the East. This guy's really smelly because he's been out with the sheep for quite some time."

"Bring him," Samuel replied. "Let me look at him."

So Jesse sent for his youngest son. When Samuel saw Jesse's youngest son walk into the house, a little boy, he began to unscrew the lid of his vase. "I think I have found the guy I'm looking for," Samuel said. (Notice that God choose the son who was out working. He was busy. God chooses busy people.)

Most of us are like Jesse. We look, but we don't see. Were you the black sheep in your family? (You know God likes sheep.) Has your family told you that you are a nobody? Have you been put off and put out and told so many times that you will amount to nothing that you have begun to believe it? Do you *feel* like the black sheep?

You are probably the one God is waiting for in the house. God sees things deep within you that others can't see. They look at you and see a nobody; God looks at you and sees a worthwhile somebody. You may spend your whole life competing with others—trying to prove that you are somebody—and still feel like nobody. Be free from that today! You do not have to live with that any longer. You don't have to *try* to be somebody, because you *are* somebody.

You Came Out of God

When God created the heavens and the earth, He first decided what He wanted to make something out of and then He spoke to that source. When God wanted plants He spoke to the dirt. When God wanted fish He spoke to the waters. When God wanted animals He spoke to the ground. *Whatever God spoke to became the source from which the created thing came.*

Plants thus came from the dirt, fish from the water and animals from the ground. Furthermore, plants return to the dirt, fish return to the sea and animals return to the ground when they die.

All things have the same components and essence as their source. What God created is, in essence, like the substance from which it came. That means plants are one hundred percent dirt because they came from dirt. Animals are one hundred percent dirt because they came from the ground. If we would take an animal apart, we would come up with genuine dirt. If we would put a plant under a microscope and decipher all the different components, we would find that everything in that plant is in dirt, because the plant is dirt. God called it from the dirt.

Not only are all things composed of that from which they came, they must also remain attached to that source in order to live. All things must be maintained and sustained by where they came from. The minute a plant decides it doesn't like the earth anymore, it dies. The minute the fish decide they are tired of water, they die. The minute animals decide, "We don't want to eat any more dirt," they begin to die.

Thus, whatever God created came from that to which He spoke. All things were created by God's word to a source. The source of the creation also becomes, then, the essence of that creation. All things are composed of whatever they came from and hence contain the potential of that source. That means plants only have the potential of the soil. Animals only have the potential of dirt.

**All things are composed of whatever
they came from and hence contain
the potential of that source.**

When God wanted fish, He spoke to the water. When He wanted animals, He spoke to the dirt. When God created human beings, He spoke to Himself.

Then God said, "Let Us make man in Our image, in Our likeness... So God created man in His own image, in the

**image of God He created him; male and female He
created them** (Genesis 1:26-27).

God created you by speaking to Himself. You came out of
God and thus bear His image and likeness.

Look at the Inventor, Not the Invention

Never use the creation to find out who you are, because
the purpose of something is only in the mind of the One
who made it. That is one of the reasons why God has a
tremendous problem with idol worship. How can you iden-
tify your ability by worshipping a snake? How can you find
out your worth by believing that you will come back as a rat
or a roach? How dare you believe that your purpose for
existence can be discovered in a relationship with a wooden
statue? You will never know yourself by relating to the creation, only to the Creator. *The key to understanding life is in
the* source *of life, not in the life itself.*

Many of the inventions man has produced would be
misunderstood if only the invention were considered and
not the intention of the inventor. In other words, the man
who created the refrigerator had in his mind what it was
supposed to be used for. He did not intend that it should
be used for a trap in the back yard for a kid to be locked in
and die from suffocation. Even though thousands of
children have died in refrigerators, that was not the
inventor's intention.

The automobile is tearing out lamp posts all over the
world and destroying people's homes and lives. But Mr.
Ford, who first developed the assembly line to mass produce
the automobile, never thought about it that way. He was
thinking about transporting people and helping the human
race to become a mobile community. He started us to thinking about trolleys and trains and buses. The many people
who died through accidents and derailments were not part

of his intention. They were not in his mind when he designed His famous T. Ford automobile.

You Have Part of God

You will never discover who you were meant to be if you use another person to find yourself. You will never know what you can do by using what I've done to measure your ability. You will never know why you exist if you use my existence to measure it. All you will see is what I've done or who I am. If you want to know who you are, look at God. The key to understanding life is in the source of life, not in the life itself. You are who you are because God took you out of Himself. If you want to know who you are, you must look at the Creator, not the creation.

There are three words we use to describe God. First, God is omniscient—which means He is all-knowing. Second, God is omnipresent—which means God is present everywhere. Third, God is omnipotent—which means God is always potent. God is always full of power—He has in Him the potential for everything. From the beginning, God gave that same ability to be potent to all His creation. He planted within each person or thing He created—including you—the ability to be much more than it is at any one moment. Thus God created you to be omni-potent.

That is not to say we are equal to God. No. What I am saying is that the word *omnipotent* relates not only to God, but to us as well. We are always full of potential. Our potential is the dormant ability, reserved power, untapped strength and unused success God designed into each of us. What I see when I look at you is not all you are. It is only what you have become so far. Your potential is much greater than what you are right now. What you will become is much more than we could ever believe now. You are somebody because you came out of God, and He leaked some of Himself into you.

God Pronounces What He Sees

How you feel or what others say about you is not important. You are who God says you are; He sees in you more than you can possibly imagine. Your potential is limited only by God, not others.

Coward or Warrior?

God came to a frightened young man named Gideon. Gideon obviously thought God was talking to someone else when the angel of the Lord called him a mighty warrior (Judges 6:12). The angel didn't say, "Oh, coward. Do you know you have strength?" Nor did the angel say, "Oh black man, do you know that you can be like the white man?" The angel just came in and announced what he saw: "Oh mighty man of war power." That means "Oh great warrior."

Think about it. Warrior? Gideon was hiding from the enemy trying to separate some wheat from the chaff so he wouldn't starve. He was doing it underground so no one could see him. When the angel said, "You are a brave man," Gideon started looking around to see who the angel was talking to.

God never tells us what others see. He never calls us what others call us. Gideon thought he was a coward. God knew him to be a great warrior and pronounced what He saw.

Flaky, Flaky

God also saw in Peter what others failed to see. His given name was Simon, which means *meek.* (Literally it means "unstable, flaky, leaf.") When Jesus met Simon, he was the flakiest, leafiest man you ever met. He was always going with the wind—changing his mind. But God saw a stone in the leaf. The first time Jesus met Peter, He changed Peter's name from Simon (leaf) to Peter (stone). Although Simon was an unstable guy, Jesus said, "I'm going to change your

name. Your name is Peter." Peter acted like a leaf throughout Jesus' earthly ministry. Still Jesus called him *rock* every
morning. Jesus saw in Peter something his mother had not
seen. He kept chipping until finally, at Pentecost, Peter's
true nature was revealed.

Stop Believing What Others Say

Too often we believe the lies we are told. We believe that
we are "no good" and worthless. Jesus says, "Not so. I came
to show you that you are more than you think you are." You
are the image of God.

God always *sees* what men and women only *look* at. In a
manger, God saw a King...in a servant, a Savior...in a
sacrifice, salvation...in a crucifixion, a resurrection. In death,
God was working at life; in defeat, He was looking at victory.
What you or I, or your country or my country, looks like is
not what God sees. God looks beyond the surface to the
potential deep within. That is God's way of thinking about
everything. Beyond the immediate troubles God sees success, and He continues to call it forth until what He sees
becomes reality.

Remember that the seed of every tree is in the fruit of
the tree. That means the blessings of the Third World nations are in the Third World nations, and the prosperity of
America is in America. When we become concerned about
our individual lives or the corporate life of our countries, we
come up with all kinds of schemes and plans to solve the
problem. But the answer is not in a multitude of systems and
programs. The answer is right inside of us. It's our attitudes
that make the difference. No one can *make you* rowdy or
careless or thoughtless. You *are* rowdy and careless and
thoughtless because you *choose* to be. So stop it! Stop being
rowdy...stop being careless...stop being thoughtless. Only

you can control how you act. You've got the potential to be considerate and sensitive.

God saw in Peter something that Peter had never seen in himself. Peter was so busy agreeing with what others called him that he missed his true potential. When we start believing what others call us, we are in big trouble. Then we throw our hands up in despair and refuse to try. People call us lazy, so we become lazy. People call us careless or stupid or clumsy, so we become careless or stupid or clumsy. Watch it! What others look at is not important. Who we are depends on what *we see*.

Do you believe you could walk into a prison and meet some of the greatest men and women in the world? Can you think that way? They made a mistake. They made a misjudgment. They made poor decisions. But that doesn't invalidate their potential. It doesn't destroy who they can be. In that jail there may be a murderer on death row. But when God looks at that person, He doesn't see a murderer; He sees an author or a leader or a great world changer.

Many times God is in disagreement with the people closest to you. He may even be in disagreement with you, because the only person God agrees with is Himself—only He knows your true potential. Have you failed? Go to God. He'll call you "success" and keep calling you "success" until you feel it. That's what Jesus did for Peter.

What Does God See in You?

I wonder what God sees as He walks around you. I'm sure He sees beautiful things in you, but you are believing what other people are saying. People say: "You are no good. You'll never be somebody." But God is saying: "I see a jewel." We are diamonds in the rough. Just keep on believing that. Keep on moving forward to your goal. Remember that there is something in you more precious than what others have said about you. The sculptor never gives up until he gets out of the rock what he sees.

There is something in you more precious than what others have said about you.

I have a piece of wooden sculpture in my home that I did about fifteen years ago. The sculpture isn't what I intended it to be because as I was chiseling out the image that I had seen in the tree, part of it was knocked off by too much pressure. Because that part dropped off, I could no longer create the image that I had intended. So I looked at the piece of wood again. I walked around it thinking, "I've gotta change my concept a little." I had to rethink how to retain the beauty of the sculpture though I had lost an important part of the wood.

Eventually, I modified my design. But I am the only person who knows that piece of sculpture was made from a modified design. The modification is not evident in the finished form. If I showed you the piece, you wouldn't even notice what I'm talking about. People have admired that piece of wood for many years. They look at it and say, "Wow! This is beautiful." And I never tell them that what they see is not what they were originally supposed to see.

That piece of sculpture sitting in my home reminds me of your life and mine. Parts of our lives have been knocked off by our past. We've done some dumb things that have messed up the beauty God intended. But look what God has done. He's saved us. Instead of discarding us because we have not turned out like He intended us to be, He has taken us—including our marred and chipped and rusted and knocked off past—and formed us into something beautiful. When people see us now, they won't believe what we used to be. And God will never tell them. Hallelujah! When people look at you and think you are the best thing that ever came down the pike, don't tell them what you used to be. Just say, "Thank you very much. The Chief Sculptor had His hands on me." God can bring beauty out of your mistakes. He can take what you have messed up and bless it up. He can take the thing that seemed impossible to you and form it into something beautiful.

In every piece of stone a sculptor sees a figure. But we never see it until he takes it out. Whereas we may see only an old stump of a tree on the side of the road, a wood sculptor sees a beautiful piece that we would pay thousands of dollars to own. What looks like garbage to the nonartistic person is a treasure to the artist.

Christ Is in You

I wonder what God sees when he looks at you. I believe He sees Christ. When God looks at you, He does not see you. He sees Christ. Paul, when writing to the Colossian church, proclaimed that God had chosen to make known a mystery.

To them God has chosen to make known among the Gentiles the glorious riches of this mystery, which is Christ in you, the hope of glory (Colossians 1:27).

The mystery is *that Christ is in you.* That is your hope of glory. This suggests, then, that our task is not to get Christ *into* us, but *out of* us. Please get this into your minds. *What God sees when He looks at you is Christ.*

**Our task is not to get Christ *into* us,
but *out of* us.**

Most of us want to be like Jesus. That's not what God wants. God wants us to be like Christ. Jesus came to show us what Christ looks like when He takes on human form. But it is Christ that God's looking at. God sees Christ in you. That's the hope of glory—*Christ in you*. Let me explain.

Christ is the image of God. The word *image* does not mean "a statue of something." It means "the essence of the being." Christ is the image of God. That means when God created you, He created you in His image, and His image is Christ. That's why the Bible never calls us the Body of Jesus. Jesus was the human manifestation of the heavenly Christ. We humans on earth, with all our fallibilities and weaknesses—God pronounces on us: "You are the body of Christ."

In other words, Christ is in us somewhere. Christ is in me. Christ is in you. God knows He is there. His image is there. So God called us Christ.

If we go to God and say, "God, please introduce me to your people," God will say, "Sure. Here is Christ." But we'll say, "No. No. No. I want to meet Christ," to which God will reply, "Sure. Here's Christ" as He shows us the Church. When we want to meet Christ, God will show us the Church. But we can't accept this because we think Christ is in heaven. No, He isn't. Jesus is in heaven. Christ is sitting in your clothes, living in the body of the believer. Christ is the essence of God—He's God Himself.

God intended for you to be created in His image. Although you may say, "I want to be like Jesus," God says, "There's something deeper." You were lost and Jesus came to bring you back. God sent Jesus so you could see yourself.

God already knows who He is—He doesn't need your praise to make Him feel like God. God doesn't need you to tell Him how great He is—He knew it before you ever thought of praising Him. God wants you to know who you are—who you were supposed to look like. He's after the real person buried under the cap of your sin. Your IQ doesn't measure who you are, God does. Your true IQ is spelled *H-O-L-Y S-P-I-R-I-T,* because you have what God is. Christ is in you. That's who you are.

PRINCIPLES

1. All things have the same components and essence as their source.

2. When God created human beings, He spoke to Himself.

3. You will never know yourself by relating to the creation, only to the Creator.

4. Your potential is much greater than what you are right now.

5. Your potential is limited only by God, not others.

6. God sees Christ in you.

4 | What Happened to the Real You?

**When man puts a limit on what he can be,
he has put a limit on what he will be.**

In the beginning, God created man by speaking to Himself. He took a little bit of Himself and put it into the first man so Adam would be like Him and could share in His life.

But the life God intended for His children was destroyed by their disobedience. Satan's deception and the sin of the man and the woman destroyed the relationship between God and the creatures He had taken out of Himself. The fellowship of like thoughts and purposes was broken, and man's relationship with God became distorted and skewed. Human beings lost their potential to be like the Creator—to know His thoughts and see through His eyes. Through sin, our access to God was cut off and the wealth of God's secret wisdom was buried. The deep things of God became more than we could know or comprehend.

Satan came into our lives to minimize, nullify and destroy our potential. He has killed, stolen and destroyed what God planted deep within each person. Through the years, the devil has succeeded in convincing men and women, each with a little part of God, that they are worthless, rotten, incapable people. But in the fullness of time Jesus came into the world to address this very problem.

The reason the Son of God appeared was to destroy the devil's work (1 John 3:8).

Jesus came to wage "the battle of the caps"—*the battle of the destroyers.* There are two destroyers in the world. One is satan; the other is Jesus. Satan comes to destroy, and Jesus comes to destroy.

Do You Want to Be Like God?

Satan is God's enemy and ours. He is our adversary, out to blind us to the truth of God's love and the wisdom that offers us hope. Anything that is destructive—anything that steals something from you or destroys something that belongs to you—is from the enemy. He is a destruction mechanism that comes to destroy, kill and steal. But what is he destroying? First satan destroyed man's potential to be like his Creator. Satan said to Adam, "Do you want to be like God? Pick that fruit." The man and woman already were like God; but by following the advice of satan they were destroyed. Their potential to be like God was clogged up right then when they failed—it was capped off.

God's Holding Back on You

Satan continued to work his art of deception when he said, "God is hiding something from you." He destroyed Adam and Eve's concept of God. To the man and the woman, God became Someone who was holding back on them. Satan said, "God doesn't want you to know what He knows." What do you mean God didn't want Adam and Eve to know what He knew? Adam and Eve were *born* related in spirit with God. God *created* them to know Him. Thus, satan stole both man's potential to be like God and his understanding of God.

Aren't You Ugly!

The deceiver also distorted man's self-concept. He said to them: "Look at you. You are naked." So the man and woman felt bad about themselves and they put on clothes. They tried to cover up their bodies.

Ever since that day, we have become professional *"cover-ups."* We don't like ourselves. We don't like our physical bodies. Yuk! I don't like how skinny I am...how fat I am...how my hair grows...how my eyes are...how my lips are. I don't like my black, brown, red, yellow or white skin. So we try to cover up what we don't like. It is strange how we work on things. If our hair is curly, we straighten it. If our skin is too pale, we get a tan. We don't like what we are. Nobody is satisfied with themselves. We all walk around saying, "Why do you want to be like me? I want to be like you."

We have become professional "cover-ups."

This attitude is from the devil. We can't just be ourselves because satan has destroyed our appreciation of what God made. Our potential has been distorted so that we don't want to be black or tall or fat. We don't want to have curly hair or fat lips or small eyes. We have accepted satan's ploy to destroy our esteem for the beautiful creation God made us to be.

Satan, who comes to destroy everything God created, has destroyed our concepts of ourselves. Because we do not like ourselves, we do all kinds of dumb things. If you love yourself, you are not going to lower your standards. You will not sell yourself to anybody. You won't allow anybody to buy you—you are too expensive.

Come On—Get Smart!

Satan also came to destroy our real intelligence. In the garden a strange word is used in the Hebrew to talk about knowing. The Bible says Adam and Eve *knew* that they were naked (Genesis 3:7). *Knew* means they "became physically—or sensually—aware." Their senses suddenly took on leadership. Thus the soul became alive without the spirit directing it. Man began to live from the outside, instead of the inside. Adam and Eve became aware of their nakedness. They became aware of the leaves that could be used to cover themselves. They became conscious of shame and fear—the things that come from the outside, from the intellect.

Satan destroyed man's true intelligence, which is a spiritual relationship with God. When we are connected with God, our spirits can know anything. That's why the knowledge God communicates is not learned. It is discerned. The knowledge of God isn't found in any book; it's a deeper knowledge. Your real intelligence is not studied; it is discerned. Wow!

**Your real intelligence is not studied;
it is discerned.**

When man lost his relationship with God, he became a victim of education. He began to look to books and movies and the words of others—what he can see, hear, taste, feel and touch—to gain knowledge. Those things became our sources of information. When satan destroyed our real intelligence, we looked outside ourselves to find knowledge.

You'll Never Be Anything

By destroying our relationship with God, satan capped off our life potential. He continually destroys any possibility that we might become more than we already are: He puts teachers in our classrooms to call us stupid. He sends brothers and sister to call us dumb and "no good." He gives us parents who tell us, "You'll never be anything."

Satan sets us up. He anoints your mother to call you a bastard. He sets her up to cap off what you are. Satan chops up your self-confidence and slams the door on your potential by convincing you that you are nothing: "You'll never rise above your family's status. You'll never go beyond where your neighborhood took you. You'll never be any more than your mom and your pa. You don't stand a chance." The devil has been teaching and preaching that to keep us down. He is very skilled at this deceptive art.

What You Have Isn't Life

But Jesus came to destroy satan's lies. He came to free us from those things that retard, distort and short-circuit everything we are capable of being and doing. He said,

I am come that they might have life, and might have it abundantly (John 10:10 NAS).

"Okay. That's fine. I have life now."

"But no, that's not enough. I came that you may have an *abundance* of life."

We think life is what we have now. No! In the Greek, the same word is used for *abundance* as is used for *fountain*. Jesus came to take the cap off your well...to unclog the true you...to open up the capacity of who you are and who you can be. We are going to have an oil spill. This thing is going to explode. Jesus didn't come just to take off your well cover. He came to start an explosion of water—a potential welling up and never stopping. He said,

> **Whoever believes in Me, as the Scripture has said, streams of living water will flow from within him** (John 7:38).

> **...whoever drinks the water I give him will never thirst. Indeed, the water I give him will become in him a spring of water welling up to eternal life** (John 4:14).

Jesus came so we can have fountains of life. Man, that's impressive to me!

That means until we get saved, we don't have any life. If you just became born again, you are finally getting back to your real self. All you have done for the last ten years that made you think you were somebody is but a trickle. You haven't changed the world, man. You haven't changed a man's life for eternity yet. You haven't touched a young boy for eternal life yet. You've put clothes on the boy's back, but you haven't put anything on his spirit. You haven't done anything yet! But there is a fountain, an abundance of life, welling up in you so you can do and be something. It begins when you return to your Source through Jesus Christ.

Uncapping the Well

Satan is the destroyer who comes to kill and steal and destroy. No one in the world stifles and clogs up and caps your potential like the devil does. He comes with a scheme to make you believe you can be nothing more than you have already seen. Jesus came to destroy this scheme. He came to unclog you and show you your true self. He's the best destroyer I know. I love this destroyer.

First John 3:8 says that Jesus came into the world *to destroy* the works of the devil. The work of the devil is to kill and steal and destroy—he delights in capping off our potential. The work of Jesus is to tear off the cap—opening up what satan closed. Jesus came to do exactly the opposite of what satan has done. Jesus came, not to convince God of anything, but to convince us about who we really are. His job is to put us back in touch with what God put within us at birth.

Jesus came, not to convince God of anything, but to convince us about who we really are.

What does it mean to destroy the works of the devil? How does Jesus do His job? Jesus reverses what satan has done. Whatever Jesus undoes, satan did. Whatever works Jesus does, satan undid it first.

For example, when Jesus took sickness from a person's body, He undid the works of the devil. Thus the work of the devil was to put the sickness into that body. When Jesus took away our sins, He destroyed the devil's work of convincing us to sin. If Jesus fed hungry people, then it must mean that satan brings poverty and hunger. If Jesus opened the eyes of the blind, then satan must close them. Jesus came to destroy the works of the devil. Whatever He did destroyed satan's previous works. Thus when Jesus says, "Everything is possible if you'll just believe" (Mark 9:23), He is reversing the lies satan has fed us. Jesus came to destroy satan's destruction.

The Cap and the Crowbar

Satan tells you that you aren't going to amount to anything: "You aren't going to be anything...you can't do anything...you will always be what you now are." Jesus comes to undo that. He says, "You can be anything you think." Jesus rips the top right off your capped well. He says, "Go ahead, gush forth."

Thus, a tremendous struggle between two destroyers goes on within us—one destroyer uses a cap, the other a crowbar. Every time the one with the crowbar yanks the top off, the other guy runs around with the cap. The minute we give him a chance, he covers us up again. The struggle is continual. Each day we experience the tension.

Jesus says, "You are saved." Satan says, "You aren't saved." Jesus says, "You are healed." Satan says, "But you still feel the pain." Jesus says, "You are free from drugs." Satan says, "You are hooked for life."

Jesus came to reverse what the devil has done. The devil came to destroy our potential. He distorts, retards, short-circuits and caps off that which God has placed within us. He uses sin to clog up our potential capacity.

What's Clogging Your Well?

Are there things in your life that have been holding you back from the things you should be doing? Are you a potential leader in your community but you're full of alcohol and you're lying in the gutter? Has cocaine stolen your potential to be the top student in your class? Is your brain all messed up so you can't even think any more? Are you in danger of being kicked out of school though you were an A student before you took the stuff? Have you run off with a dumb guy and gotten pregnant? Do you have to drop out of school and give up your visions of becoming a doctor or a lawyer, a scientist or an agricultural expert? Has sin clogged up your potential?

Did you have a business that was going well, with limitless potential, until somebody said to you, "I want you to sell some drugs for me. You'll make a lot more than you do in this business"? So you became greedy. You went ahead and sold the drugs—only you were caught and now you have a record and your business is destroyed.

Sin clogs our potential. It messes up the plan God has for each of our lives. It takes away the "And they lived happily ever after" and replaces it with "And they struggled but didn't make it through the day." Don't let that be the last chapter in the book God has written on you. God sent Jesus to die for you, not for Himself. Jesus knows *His* potential. He doesn't need to find out what it is. God doesn't have any problem with His potential. He is omnipotent. The problem is that *you* don't know *your* potential. You have been destroyed by the devil, and sin is stunting your growth.

Sin clogs up our potential. It messes up the plan God has for each of our lives.

Jesus came, not to die for Himself, but for you, so you could be reconnected with the Source of Life. For this reason Jesus came into the world—to destroy the works of the devil that are holding you down. Jesus came to uncap your well. He gave His life to restore your relationship with God—to give you abundant, flowing, gushing life.

PRINCIPLES

1. Satan destroyed man's potential to be like his Creator.

2. Satan distorted man's self-concept—his esteem for the beautiful creation God made him to be.

3. Satan destroyed man's true intelligence, which is a spiritual relationship with God.

4. When Satan crippled man's real intelligence, man looked outside himself to find knowlege.

5. Sin clogs our potential.

6. Jesus came to bring us abundant, refreshing, new life.

5 | Whose Wisdom?

Wisdom is supreme; therefore get wisdom.
Proverbs 4:7

Wisdom protects us from the dangers of knowledge.

Potential is dormant ability. (The word *dormant* literally means "that which is, but it is just lying there below its full strength, unused.") It is also reserved power, untapped strength and unused success. Potential is everything that a thing is, that has not yet been seen or manifested. Everything in life begins as potential. All things have the potential to fulfill themselves, because God created everything with potential. There is no fulfillment in life without understanding the reason for being. If we want to know the real potential of something, we first have to know what that thing was created to do.

So if you have a seed in your hand, an ear of corn or a pea, you will never get the seed's complete fulfillment until you know that there is a plant inside that seed. It is only as we look beyond the seed to the plant that we understand its true potential.

The same is true of our relationship with God. God created each man with a great wealth of potential. Too often, however, we look only at what we presently have. We look at our last dollar and say, "All I have is one dollar."

But God says, "No. That is not all you have. If you only knew the potential of that dollar."

And we reply, "But God you don't understand. There's a one next to that '$' thing."

Again God says, "No. If you could just take this dollar and put it into a certain condition, it would multiply."

The potential of everything is related to its purpose for being. Before we can understand the potential of a thing or person, we first must know the conditions under which it was meant to exist. Thus the most important thing for you and me, as human beings, is to try and find out for the rest of our lives what is the purpose for everything in life. That is our main goal. Unless we ask ourselves, "What is the purpose for everything in life?" we will die without having experienced the potential of everything. We will miss the wisdom of God in creation.

The apostle Paul, in the first chapter of First Corinthians, describes the wisdom of the world and the wisdom of God.

> Where is the wise man? Where is the scholar? Where is the philosopher of this age? has not God made foolish the wisdom of the world? For since in the wisdom of God the world through its wisdom did not know Him, God was pleased through the foolishness of what was preached to save those who believe. Jews demand miraculous signs and Greeks look for wisdom, but we preach Christ crucified: a stumbling block to Jews and foolishness to Gentiles... (1 Corinthians 1:20-22)

When somebody tells you they are wise, don't get carried away. Although they may have wisdom, it might not be the right kind of wisdom.

The Wisdom of the World

Did you know that satan still has wisdom? Ezekiel 38:20 tells us that satan's wisdom became corrupted. God could not take back what He had given, so satan is still wise. But his wisdom is corrupt.

Before the fall, Lucifer's responsibility in heaven was to be the music and worship leader. He was designed with the potential not only to lead in music and worship, but also to produce it. Lucifer's body was made with pipes in it so that every time he lifted a wing, a sound came out—music. He never taught an orchestra because the orchestra arrived when he did. As soon as he started fanning his wings, the angels started singing. This guy was a beautiful angel. He had the potential to lead all heaven, that other world out there, into worship and music. But that wisdom became corrupted. It was not taken from him, it just got corrupted. God is the Creator, but satan is the perverter. God creates everything; satan creates nothing. But everything God creates, satan perverts.

That's why music is such an important part of our world today. The guy who is running the spirit of the world is a cheap musician. The amounts of money the devil uses to support the music ministry of the world is amazing. Michael Jackson alone made two hundred and twenty million dollars last year. Whitney Houston made eighty-four million dollars—in just one year. And the Church can't raise even one million. Although that may sound strange, it is possible because the cheap musician who fell is the one who is backing the music industry. He is manipulating that stuff. He knows just what to do. But God still has the final word, and I like what He has done. God has put music into the Church and into us. He now calls for praise from man. But the point is, satan's potential is related to his purpose.

What Is Wisdom?

In First Corinthians, Paul scoffs: "Where are you, those who think you are wise? Is not your wisdom just so much foolishness?" Attacking the supposed wisdom of the world, the apostle declares that it is foolishness. God, in His wisdom, has made the wisdom of the world to be just so much folly (1 Corinthians 1:20).

God considers foolishness any wisdom that does not fulfill its original purpose. So if you are wise and you can really figure things out, but you use it to steal, God says, "You are foolish." If you are a very skillful musician, but you use it to create lewdness and sensuality, and to cause people to go into perversion, then God calls that foolishness. If you know that the power you have to believe was given to you by God, but you prefer to believe there is no God, God calls you a fool. For when you use the belief God has given to you to say you don't believe in Him, your wisdom becomes foolishness. The fool says in his heart, "There is no God." He takes the ability God gave him to believe and uses that belief power to not believe in God. God says, "That's foolishness!"

**God considers foolishness any wisdom
that does not fulfill its original purpose.**

Although God calls the wisdom of the world foolishness, it is still wisdom. It's a perverted wisdom used by the chief of perverters to blind us to its very foolishness. For who could believe God would use a crucifixion to bring salvation to the world. That is not the way we expect Him to work. We look for miraculous signs and unusual insights to indicate the presence and working of God. What wisdom would choose a poor carpenter to bring the greatest gift the world has ever known? Surely not the wisdom of the world, which looks to the wealthy and the well-educated. But for those who believe in Jesus Christ, God's apparent foolishness is revealed as true wisdom. The wisest of human thoughts appears puny beside this foolishness of God, and the greatest of man's strengths pales beside Christ's weakness. What is a stumbling block or pure foolishness for those who don't believe in Christ stands, for the Christian, as a towering source of truth, strength and hope. *That* is wisdom.

Your Secret Wisdom

God has given you a secret wisdom that He placed in you before you were born. He planted within you a potential something—a wisdom to know who you are and what you were created to be and do. That potential something was in God, but He allowed it to leak into you when He pulled you out of Himself. It's a hidden understanding that follows neither the wisdom of our society nor the insights of our leaders. Unlike the wisdom of the world, which is worthless, God's secret wisdom about you is a priceless jewel.

Many people die without unveiling their wealth of wisdom. They die in total foolishness, without experiencing the life that dwells within. What a pity! They have missed God's secret wisdom. (*Secret* here does not mean "to be withheld from." It rather has the meaning of "to have never known existed." There is a difference. God is not holding back from the world. He is not withholding from us our true potential. It's just that we have never known that it is within us.) They have missed the wisdom God designed before the beginning of time for the honor of man.

> We do, however, speak a message of wisdom among the mature, but not the wisdom of this age or of the rulers of this age, who are coming to nothing. No, we speak of God's secret wisdom, a wisdom that has been hidden and that God destined for our glory before time began (1 Corinthians 2:6-7).

This wisdom is like a secret that was supposed to be known before we were created. It's a wisdom from God that He is keeping for us. It was in God and now it dwells in *us*. In other words, you were born with wisdom that literally came out of God. You have the ability to line up with God. You are in the God class.

You were born with wisdom that literally came out of God.

I know you may find that hard to accept—perhaps you think I am a mad man. But the truth is you'll be shocked when you understand who you really are. You don't know what you have inside that you are selling so cheaply. You have God's secret wisdom, a wisdom that you should be using to discover the earth.

None of the rulers of this world understand it, nor have they ever understood it. If only we could understand who we are (and I guess I include Christians, because we used to be there, and we need to find out where we used to be). We keep thinking that the life we left behind is better than the life toward which we are headed. We are constantly dipping into the ways and wisdom of the world to try and solve our present situations. But the world does not know the wisdom and potential God has already destined for us. They don't understand it, because if they had understood it they would not have crucified the Lord Jesus!

"No eye has seen, no ear has hear, no mind has conceived what God has prepared for those who love Him"—but God has revealed it to us by His Spirit (1 Corinthians 2:9-10).

Your eyes can't see, your ears can't hear, neither can your mind imagine what God intends for His children. It's totally beyond what you can understand. If you could see through your eyes what you were created to be, you'd change your life. If you could hear through your ears or perceive through your mind... But the Scriptures say you can't. Your situation sounds hopeless: No eyes have seen it...no ears have heard it...no mind has conceived it. Your eyes and ears and mind cannot help you understand what God prepared for you before you were born. If they could, you'd shape up!

The Deep Things of God

"But God has revealed it to us by His Spirit." *But* indicates a change. *But* inserts hope in the midst of hopelessness. Most people do not know what God intends for their lives. They have not seen their secret wisdom, nor have they heard about it. They have never even thought about the stuff because there are certain things we cannot understand unless the Holy Spirit reveals them to us. They are so deep within our potential that we need help to drag them out.

God had those deep things within Him before He made us; He put them into us at birth. But we don't know they exist because sin has clogged up the entry way. It is as if God struck a well and put wealth in it—a wealth of oil. Wealth is under there in your bosom. There is wealth in your personality—wealth in your being. But it has been clogged up and capped off by sin.

When you were born, the cap over your potential was firmly in place. Outside God's grace you will never know what is buried beneath that cap. Billions of dollars of wealth are buried within you, but you are not aware of it. You're walking along cool, but you don't know who you are. You don't understand that what you see is merely the shadow of your potential. That's why the Bible says, "nor has it entered the hearts of man the things God has under the cap for him." Oh, man!

The Holy Spirit Connection

In His mercy, God has placed within each of us the answer to this dilemma. After the resurrection of Jesus Christ, God sent the gift of the Holy Spirit. That same Spirit, which we receive at our new birth, provides the connection between our spirits and God's secret wisdom.

Your capped potential is like a new battery. You came into the world full of the ability to run the whole thing. But you're just sitting there. Your stored power isn't being used. Like a battery that needs acidic water inside it before it can really fulfill its purpose, you need something to unleash the potential locked inside you. The Holy Spirit is the key that allows all the dormant power within you to come to life. Without the filling of the Holy Spirit, you can never function to your fullest potential.

**The Holy Spirit is the key that allows
all the dormant power within you
to come to life.**

Have you ever wondered why we have to be born of the Spirit? Why does the Holy Spirit come and connect with our spirits? Think for a moment about your spirit. The deepest knowledge about ourselves comes to us through our spirits—we can't know anything deeper than our spirits reveal. No one knows more about you than you know about yourself, for who can understand a man better than his own spirit (1 Corinthians 2:11)?

If you just got saved, your spirit doesn't know anything about you. Before your new birth in Christ, you were spiritually dead. Your spirit has been paralyzed for 15, 20 or 30 years (however long it took you to get saved). You have been dumb and ignorant about who you really are, because you can't truly know yourself until you become spiritually alive.

If you are not a Christian, you don't even know who you are. Only the spirit of a man knows the real thoughts of what a man is supposed to be, and we are born spiritually dead. We will never know who we are supposed to be until we accept Jesus as our Savior and receive God's gift of His Spirit.

If then, your spirit doesn't know any more about you than what it has learned since you got saved, look at how little it knows. Just look at you. Do you know where you would be if you had not been saved?

Now don't get me wrong. You aren't perfect yet. Don't get carried away. You know there is still much that needs to be worked on—many things that need to be refined. But do you know what happens? The more we know about who we are, the more our attitude toward ouselves changes. Isn't that something? The minute we realize who we are we say, "Wait a minute now. I'm the King's kid," and we begin to put on kingly clothes. We think, "I'm a child of God now," so we start changing our language. We think, "Gosh, man. I'm a prosperous person," and we start expecting things to happen in our lives. As our knowledge about who we are grows, our lives change.

All this is possible because the Holy Spirit goes to the cap on the well of the wealth of our potential and pries it off. He comes into our lives and goes straight for the things that are clogging us up and dragging us down. Through the power of God, He pulls off that cap and starts to drill.

**The Holy Spirit comes into our lives
and goes straight for the things that are
clogging us up and dragging us down.**

King Solomon described this process like a bucket drawing water out of a deep well. The Holy Spirit is the bucket that allows us to understand the wisdom and intentions of our hearts (Proverbs 18:4). God has prepared so many deep things about who we are. Our eyes can't see them, nor can our minds conceive them, yet God is revealing them to us through His Spirit. God doesn't want us to wait until heaven to know our full potential. He didn't give birth to us so we can develop our potential in heaven. (In fact, in heaven we will already have finished maximizing our potential.) God wants us to realize here on this planet who we are. That is His purpose in creating us. We need the Holy Spirit because eyes have not seen, ears have not heard, nor has it entered the minds of men who man really is. Only the Holy Spirit searches "the deep things of God."

Some of you have received the revelation of what it cost God to love you. Others of you have not. Some of you are ready to walk into a deeper level of knowledge; others are not. God beckons you to take another step into a deeper, more relevant knowledge of your potential in Christ—though you may have been saved for years. You need to take this step because you still don't know who you are. Only the Holy Spirit can reveal this truth to you. Your eyes cannot perceive your true potential...your ears cannot hear it... neither can your mind perceive it unless the Holy Spirit gives it to the eyes and the ears and the mind. Until He does, you continue to walk around limiting your potential.

The Spirit searches all things. It's His job to search out the deep things of God and interpret them so we can understand them. Now, listen. God is deep by Himself! Trying to figure out God Himself is deep enough; but God says, "Nope! I have some deep things." Our efforts to understand God could take a million years or more. How can we possibly understand God's deep things—the great mysteries He has to share with us? Can we imagine that the source of the deep things of God might be connected to us? Can we go inside God to those things that are deep within Him?

Yes, we can! God has given us His Spirit so we can understand all the things He oozed into us.

We have not received the spirit of the world but the Spirit who is from God, that we may understand what God has freely given us (1 Corinthians 2:12).

That's mind blowing! I'm hooked on those little things that are leaking out in me—those revelations. I'm glad the Holy Spirit can go deep to show me those things about you and me that God knows and wants to share.

There are things about you, concerning who you can be, that you haven't discovered yet—holy things that only the Holy Ghost can explain. God reveals His deep things to you through the Holy Spirit because He knows you would not believe them if they were simply told to you through your mind. Your mind cannot possibly comprehend all that God has prepared for you to be.

Forget what others have told you about who you can be. That's a joke. Don't even consider it. That is not all you can be, because the deepest things you can know about yourself are not in your mind or your emotions or even in your body. They are in your spirit. The deepest things you can know about yourself are what you get from your spirit.

That's why God gives you the Holy Spirit. The Spirit goes deep inside you to capture the wealth of your potential. He pulls deep from within you the answers to your spirit's cries, showing you who you are and why He created you. You will never be fulfilled until you understand why God made you. You will only walk around confused, thinking, "There's gotta be more. There's gotta be more."

Many people get bored coming to church. They get tired of singing and tired of praying. Even fasting doesn't meet the hunger of their hearts. Why? Because there's more than coming to church...there's more than singing...there's more than praying. When you hunger for the deep things of God, a hunger that God Himself puts within you, you will not be satisfied until the Holy Spirit reveals God's secret wisdom to you. Your spirit yearns for the deep things of God that He has within Him about you. There is a deep in you crying out to the deep things in God. You will never be satisfied, even after you are saved, because there is something inside you that continually calls out for more. And the thing you are calling for is locked up in God—the wisdom of God concerning you. You will never be fulfilled until you get filled with what God has that is supposed to be in you. That's why you have to come to God. You'll never be fulfilled without God, because you are looking for what God has.

You'll never be fulfilled without God, because you are looking for what God has.

For this reason, God gives you the Holy Spirit. The only way to get out of God and into you the deep things God knows about you is through His Spirit communing with yours. The Holy Spirit searches the deep things of God—the deep things about you that you lack. God prepared and predestined those things for you before you were created. He had them in Himself and gave them to you at birth. But you don't know those things exist, because sin has capped the well and blocked the way. Only God, through the Holy Spirit, can reveal them again.

Do you want to know how cute you can be? Check God out. Do you want to know how smart you are? Go back to God. Your potential is buried in God. We think going to the moon is great—we should see what God had planned that we didn't follow. Our eyes will never see the stuff God prepared for us, nor will our ears hear it. Only the Holy Spirit can reveal to us the deep things of God that tell us who we are.

Through the gift of the Holy Spirit, you can reestablish your relationship with God. The Holy Spirit, connected with your spirit, unravels the knots that have bound your thoughts, removes the streaks that have blurred your vision and clears the debris that has hidden your potential. Working like a sculptor, He brings out the beauty hidden deep within your being, because that is the real you.

Open your life to Jesus Christ. Allow God to reveal His secret wisdom concerning you. See with your eyes and hear with your ears things you have never seen or heard before. Conceive with your mind thoughts that never before have occurred to you. Cooperate with the Holy Spirit as He sucks out of God and into you the depths of the riches that God prepared for you. Live the rest of your life building an atmosphere where it is possible for the Holy Spirit to use you as He takes His bucket of hope, dips it deep into the wells of your potential and pulls it to the top of your senses. Drink deeply, growing in the knowledge of who you really are in God. That's my dream.

PRINCIPLES

---

1. The potential of everything is related to its purpose for being.

2. The wisdom of the world is a foolish, corrupt wisdom.

3. For those who believe, Jesus Christ is both the power and the wisdom of God.

4. God has given you a wisdom that He placed in you before you were born.

5. You are in God's class.

6. You will never know who you are supposed to be until you accept Jesus as your Savior and receive the gift of God's Spirit.

6 | Why Were You Born?

No one can make you feel inferior without your consent.

Eleanor Roosevelt

The people I have met who are progressing in life and affecting other people's lives—people like Dale Carnegie, a tremendous man who has touched many people's lives, or Robert Schuler, who is ministering to people all over the world to help them improve their self-esteem—all seem to say the same thing: If you feel good about yourself, you will feel good about other people. In other words, only after you see yourself as a worthwhile person can you appreciate others as worthwhile people.

**If you feel good about yourself,
you will feel good about other people.**

That's a very important insight because many people do not feel good about themselves. They look at themselves and wonder why God made them; or they doubt that anyone can find any good in them. But remember, God sees what others, and we ourselves, can't see. God looks at us and sees that we are worth feeling good about. We are special to God. We are valuable and important.

God Planned Your Life

The crowning work of creation came on the sixth day when God created human beings. As He looked around Him, God pronounced His creation to be good. That includes you! God looked at the man and the woman He had made and declared them to be "very good."

God has a good attitude toward you. He created you in His image and drew you out of Himself. Before you were born, you were in God. Part of His potential has been placed within you.

Do you remember the verse we suggested could be considered as the first verse in the Bible? Before the beginning was, God is (Genesis 1:0). God is so big He began the beginning. There could not be a beginning without God, because God got start started. Before start started, however, God had a finished plan for your life. Your potential is not a trial and error experience. God designed and predetermined you to be a success story.

God designed and predetermined you to be a success story.

Psalm 139 tells us that God planned each of your days before you were even born. Before you were formed, God knew you. He took great care in creating you. No part of your being was made without God's knowledge and careful concern. God wants each of us. He gives us what no other part of His creation received: His breath of life (Genesis 2:7).

You Are Not a Mistake

Have you ever felt like you were a mistake? Have your parents told you they wished you had never been born? Are you a child whose parents have told you: "I wish you would have died when you were a baby"?

You may have come into this world as the result of a rape. Your mother may have hated you in the womb because you reminded her of a man she wished to forget. But the fact that you were conceived is more important than how you were conceived. People go around dealing with *how* things happened, but God is simply concerned with *the fact* that He allowed your conception to happen.

Now when I say *allow,* I'm talking about the fact that you were conceived. You may be a bastard, conceived out of wedlock. Being omnipotent, God had the power to prevent your conception. Yet God allowed it because He wanted you to show up. You are here because God wanted you to be born. How you came isn't important. What matters is that you are here. And if you are here, God created you with care (Psalm 139:13).

**You are here because
God wanted you to be born.**

King David doesn't describe your mother in Psalm 139— she may have been an old alcoholic or a drug addict, a bastard or a prostitute. He is concerned with *you.* He describes how God knit you together in your mother's womb without describing what that womb was like. The womb in which you were knit together is no longer important. *You* are important. Your very existence means God wants you to exist. You are somebody special simply because you were born.

God saw you in your mother's womb when you were a tiny baby—a one-centimeter embryo. He looked into the secret place in your mother's womb and saw you. From the second your father's sperm and your mother's egg joined to form a child, God tenderly created you and watched you grow. God never would have allowed the sperm and the egg to come together if He had not planned for you to be born.

My frame was not hidden from You when I was made in the secret place. When I was woven together in the depths of the earth, Your eyes saw my unformed body (Psalm 139:15-16).

Although some parents feel their baby is a mistake, their thoughts are not true. God planned for that baby to be born. The manner in which the child was conceived may not have been in God's plan, but the child himself is surely part of God's plan.

Those of you who were brought up in a nice family with a mother and a father who love you may not understand those who have been put down by their family since the day of their birth. You may not understand how important it is for them to know that they are not mistakes. Be patient with them. Help them to see that God designed them long before they were born! Every child who comes into this world comes as a setup from God. That little boy or girl doesn't need to arrive to see what is going to happen, because the happening was already set up before he or she came.

God Has a Book on You

All the days ordained for me were written in Your book before one of them came to be (Psalm 139:16).

God designed you to be somebody. He looked at your unformed body and declared, "This child is good." All His plans for your life were set out long before you took a breath. He wrote out the order of your days before you lived even one day (Psalm 139:16). There's a book on you. Some chapters God wrote about you haven't even been touched yet.

Some of you are playing around in the index or you have spent years in the table of contents. Perhaps you are thirty years old and you still don't know God's plan for your life. That's playing around on the contents page. You are thirty years old and still wondering what you are supposed to be. You haven't even started yet.

Others have jumped ahead of God's plan. Though His design calls for you to be married in chapter seventeen, you got married in chapter two. You have ignored the things God wanted you to learn and experience in chapters two through sixteen so you would be prepared for marriage in chapter seventeen. You have missed out on many experiences and discoveries because you moved ahead of God's schedule.

Some people are so busy peeking into chapter seventeen they don't have time to live chapters two and three and four... Or perhaps you have pulled chapter seventeen into chapter two so that the rest of the book is destroyed. You will never have the opportunity to experience all the chapters if you pull parts of later chapters into the early ones.

God Offers You a Rewrite

God wants to take you back to the beginning, because His plans far outreach your plans. His design for your life is so great that King David describes it as *vast* (Psalm 139:17). You are thinking about being a teacher while God wants you to open a school. You have plans to be a clerk while God wants you to own the store. You want to work in a neighboring town while God wants you to go to Africa. You often cheat yourself because you don't realize the potential you have. Why settle to be a doorman when God wants you to own the house? David says it this way: "God, when I look at your thoughts in the book on me, it's like all the sands in the ocean. Your thoughts are endless. I can't fathom your confidence in me."

God designed you to live out the careful plans He prepared for you. You are made in God's image. The plan He wrote for you is perfect and right. No detail or part is missing. You have the potential to live out all that God has planned for your life—but only if you accept Jesus Christ as your Savior and Lord. That's the first step toward understanding why you were born.

Though you've messed up God's perfect plan for your life, He graciously offers to write another book for you. It probably won't be the best-seller the first book was designed to be, but at least God gives you the chance to start over. He comes and puts you back in chapter one so you can live the many details of His plan. That's what being born again is all about. It's the opportunity to start over—it's finally getting back to the first chapter of God's book on you. God has great plans for you—that's why He gave you life. Self-acceptance is the key to healthy self-esteem. Accept yourself as God made you. Allow His power to transform your weakness, rather than belittling yourself when you make mistakes.

Born to Expose His Nature

Not only did God carefully plan for the details of your life, He also determined how your life would fit into His total plan for man. Part of the answer to the why of our birth is revealed in God's desire that we should show forth His glory. The glory of God is the excess of His nature. It's all the potential of our omnipotent God that has not yet been revealed. He's full of so much more than we can think or imagine and He's waiting to use us to realize that potential.

Now to Him who is able to do immeasurably more than all we ask or imagine, according to His power that is at work within us, to Him be glory in the church and in Christ Jesus throughout all generations, for ever and ever! Amen (Ephesians 3:20-21).

Throughout the Bible, God tells us to make His name great in the earth. Praise and thanks are due God's name, which is great and awesome (Psalm 44:8, 99:3). His name is to be proclaimed among the nations (Malachi 1:11) as well as in Israel (Psalm 76:1). His name is holy (Luke 1:49; Psalm 99:3) and mighty in power (Jeremiah 10:6). Everything is done for "His name's sake." To understand this concept, we must also understand that the Hebrew concept of "name" literally is synonymous with the object. In other words, the name of the thing *is* the thing. Therefore, the name of God is Himself, and He is His name. To glorify His name, then, means exposing His nature.

God created *you* to bring glory to His name. His predestined plan for *your* life was designed to bring Him glory. He knows there is more to you than we can see because He placed part of Himself in you. His plan for your life is part of His creative work—through you God wants to continue the birth of His potential. Because you share God's omnipotent nature, Jesus said you can do even greater things than He did, if you only believe (Mark 11:23).

Knock the Limits off Your Life

The concept of Mark chapter 11 is that if you ask anything—if you can believe what you desire hard enough—God says it will be done. Somehow God gives us a little glimpse into our potential. He comes into our situation as if He's disturbed. God is disappointed in the human race. It's almost as though God looks at the ideas He stored in us and says with a voice of disappointment, "If you only knew what you can do." That's the attitude of God toward you and me.

God is totally disappointed in us because He knows what we can do. But we don't. And so He says to us: "All things are possible if you'd just believe, dummy." He's always knocking the limits off our lives.

Too often we are not willing to *believe* like God defines believe. God does not say, "Everything is possible if you get the idea." Things don't become reality because we have an idea. We have to believe in the idea. We have to believe we can do it by committing ourselves to it—abandoning ourselves to it—even if it costs us our lives. That's what it takes to believe in the Lord Jesus Christ—to lose our lives...to abandon ourselves. We must say, "I'm going to go into eternity believing in Jesus. I'm not sure what's out there, but I'm going to ride on that Name and that atonement."

God isn't impressed by your dreams. Most of us never wake up long enough to do anything with our dreams. You may have great dreams for your life, but you prefer to stay asleep because when you wake up reality says, "Okay, let's get to work." It's easier to dream an idea than to work it out. Everything is possible if you will abandon yourself to an idea enough that you are willing to lose your life for it. Thinking is great. But all things are possible when we *believe*. Jesus said in Mark chapter eleven, "Whatever you *desire* when you pray, believe you'll receive it, and you will have it." The word *desire* is the key. Being interested in or attracted to something is not desiring it. To *desire* means "to crave for something at the expense of losing everything."

**Everything is possible if you will
abandon yourself to an idea enough
that you are willing to lose your life for it.**

God's work in creation began with a plan. God conceived in His mind what He wanted before speaking His creations into visible form. By the time God was ready to speak, it was just a matter of taking what was in the plan and putting it on the site.

From Thought to Action

A *thought* is a silent word, so a *word* is an exposed thought. Everything in life starts in the thought form—it's a thought first. After it's said, it is no longer a thought. It becomes a word.

The next step is an *idea*. An idea is the concept of the thought—it has moved into a reality. Ideas are potentials.

The third level of operation is what I call *imagination*. Imagination changes an idea into a plan. If you have an idea it can come and go. You have many ideas in a day—what to cook, what to wear, what to do. You may decide the night before what you are going to wear in the morning and then wake up with a different idea. Ideas change. But if an idea develops into an imagination, it means the idea has become a plan. It is still not written or drawn, but it is in your head. Imagination is therefore a plan that is not documented. It is a visual display of your thoughts and ideas. Ephesians 3:20 challenges us to believe God is able and willing to do *"exceeding abundantly far beyond all we can think or imagine."* He dares us to use our imaginations.

If you want to be successful in life, take your ideas and turn them into imagination; then take imagination and duplicate it physically. Put it down. Let it become a plan of action.

Followers, Dreamers, Visionaries and Missionaries

Many people never get beyond the idea stage. That's sad. They are usually followers. The people who get to the imagination stage often talk a lot but they do nothing. They are dreamers. But when a man or woman takes his imagination and puts it on paper, you are looking at a visionary who is becoming a missionary. Visionaries see great things in their minds. Many visionaries are in the graveyard. They had visions, but their visions never made it to mission. When a visionary becomes a missionary, you have a man or woman who is going to change the world.

Make Plans...Set Goals

God wants us to become people who have plans. He says, "Use your imagination. I won't give you a thought if you can't do it. If you think it, I'm ready to do it." Plans are documented imaginations. If you can document an imagination, you've developed a plan for action.

If you are having problems in your life, I mean real problems, you probably don't have a piece of paper on which you have documented your plans for the next five years. If you are disillusioned with life—bored and confused—I can almost guarantee that you don't know what is going on in your life. You're just living from day to day in the absence of a concrete, documented plan by which to live. You've been dealing with the same issues and habits and struggles for years. You slide forward a little only to slide backward again. Whenever things get hard, you start reminiscing about "the good old days" and fall back into habits you had conquered.

If there is no goal in front of you, you'll check the hazardous holes behind you. If there is no vision in front of you to pull you on, you will be dragged back to the path you know well. If your imagination does not become documented, it will soon ferment into vapor and disillusionment.

Let me explain. If you do not have a paper on which you have written a general plan for your life, you may decide something one minute only to change it five minutes later. You will be confused, disoriented, misguided and frustrated.

Progress requires a plan of action. Ideas must be put down if they are to influence the way you live.

Many of us plan our meals for the next week, but we have nothing planned for our lives. The food we eat just goes away—it doesn't touch the future.

Stop. Set your course. Imagine into your future as far as you can. Chart what you are going to do for the next five months...twelve months...two years. Start imagining what you want to be...what you want to accomplish...where you want to go...who you want to influence. Do something and then put your plan in a convenient location so you can check your progress, seeing how close you are to your next goal.

You will be amazed how that will make you work every day. It will encourage you to move. You will begin to see God's power at work within you, and that will motivate you even more. Don't worry how you are going to meet all your goals. God says, "You make the plan and I will give the answer how it will be accomplished."

God created you to change the world. He carefully designed a plan for your life that allows you to share in His work of creation. Because you were made in God's image, you share His potential to be and do much more than is visible now. Everything you see was originally a thought in the mind of God—an invisible idea that God worked into sight. Make a plan. Give yourself something to be motivated toward. As you dream, think, imagine and plan who you want to be, you will begin to see why God created you and the work He has designed you to do. You are destined by God to reveal His glory—His very nature.

PRINCIPLES

1. You are worth feeling good about because God wanted you to be born.

2. God has a detailed plan for your life.

3. The first step in living out God's plan is accepting Jesus Christ as your Savior and Lord.

4. God created you with a part of His potential so you could expose and share in His glory.

5. God's glory is the excess of His potential—His many plans that wait to be revealed through us.

6. Develop a plan for your life that fulfills some of the possibilities God placed within you before you were born. Then believe and work them into existence.

7 | What Can You Do?

**A man cannot discover new oceans unless
he has the courage to lose sight of the shore.**

For about two years now my little boy has been coming
to me when he's trying to do something and saying, "I can't
do this." I always respond to him by saying, "There is nothing named 'can't.' " When he comes back to me and says,
"I don't know how to do it," I always reply, "There's always
a way to do everything."

Several days ago my son and I were out in the yard playing bat and ball. I was throwing the ball to him and he kept
on missing with the bat. Finally he became really upset and
said, "I can't do that," to which I replied, "There's nothing
named 'can't.' " Slowly he repeated after me, "There's nothing named 'can't.' " Then I said, "Hold the bat," and I threw
the ball. He hit the ball and then said, "There's nothing
named 'can't.' "

Several days later when I stopped by home to drop off
my daughter, my son came running and wanted to play
basketball. When I said that I had to go back to the office
to do some work, he insisted that he wanted to play ball with
me then. When I again replied that I *had* to go to the office,
he said, "There's nothing named 'can't.' "

Do you see the point? If he begins to think that way at four years of age, this world is in for a winner. Too often we fail in our efforts because we have been brought up believing that we cannot do some things. The people who change the world are people who have taken *impossible* out of their dictionaries. The men and women who make changes in history are those who come against the odds and tell the odds that it's impossible for the odds to stop them.

**The people who change the world
are people who have taken *impossible*
out of their dictionaries.**

The apostle Paul, when looking back over his years in the Lord's service, stated that he could do all things through Christ who strengthens him. The Greek terminology for *strengthen* does not mean we are weak and God comes and props us up. Paul's words literally mean: "Christ who continues to infuse me with ability." Thus Paul is saying: "I can do all things through the potential of Christ who infuses me with the ability to do all things." This strength is not a strength that comes once in a while, but a continual ability that is infused into us because we are connected to Christ. Thus our potential is not limited to doing *some* of the things God asks us to do. We can do *all things*—whatever we believe and desire to do for God. We can do this because the ability to do so is already deposited in us. The basis for this deposit of Christ's ability goes back to God's work in creation.

God is the source of all potential because everything that is was in God. He created everything with potential and gave it the ability to fulfill itself. The potential God gave is related to the source from which He took the thing. That means whatever you came out of is an indication of your potential. Thus your potential is as great as God's potential, because when God wanted you, He spoke to Himself. When He wanted plants and animals, God spoke to the ground. But when He wanted human beings, God spoke to Himself. You came out of God. Thus the limit of your potential is God.

The Demands of the Creator

Genesis chapter one also teaches us that potential is determined by the demands made on it by the creator of it. This is the most amazing thing I have ever discovered about potential. The potential of a thing is determined by the demands made on it by the one who made it. A creator will not call forth from his creation something he did not put into it.

If, for example, the Ford Motor Company wanted to build a car with an engine that was supposed to have a certain degree of horsepower to get up to 200 miles per hour, they would create a car with enough spark plugs and pistons and other things to run at that speed. First they would design it. Then they would build it. Finally they would hire a professional to take it on a test track to clock its speed. Because they designed and built the car to run at 200 miles per hour, they would tell the driver: "Run this car until it hits 200 miles per hour."

Now how can they demand from that car 200 miles per hour? Simple. They built into the car the ability to produce 200 miles per hour. If all other cars can only go 198 miles per hour, they have reason to believe their car will go into a race and win. They are calling forth from the car, or demanding of it, what they created it to produce.

Or let's think about a flight of the spaceship Challenger. The men who plan a trip into space decide before the spaceship ever leaves earth when the journey will begin, where the spaceship will go, what the crew will do while in space, how long the trip will last, and where the ship will land. The men who created the spaceship and the people who trained the astronauts know what the ship and the crew can do. The demands they make are thus consistent with their potential.

Or suppose you want to take an airplane trip. If you want to fly from Nassau to Chicago, you depend upon the expertise and knowledge of others to assure you that you will get there. You may look at the airplane and say, "This thing will never get me to Chicago," but what you believe doesn't really matter because you are not the creator of either the airplane or the flight route. The folks who build and maintain the airplane would never require it to make the trip from Nassau to Chicago if they thought the plane lacked the potential to do so. The ticket agent would never schedule you for that airplane if he knew the flight didn't go to Chicago. The potential of a thing is determined by the demands placed upon it by the creator.

God's "Money-Back" Guarantee

The same is true of our relationship with God. Whenever God demands something of you, don't ask whether you can do it. When you pick up the Bible and read that you can do anything if you believe, don't argue that you can't. God believes (in fact He knows) that whatever you believe hard enough, strong enough and committed enough can come out of you because He put it in you. Your potential, like that of any other creation, is determined by the demands of your Creator.

God also graciously offers you a "Money-Back Guarantee." When you buy an appliance, a manual usually comes with it that says: "Read this before you hook it up." It also says: "You've just purchased a television that can do XYZ." You've never seen the television do that before, but the manual says it can and will because the manufacturer made it possible for it to do it. At the end of the manual, there is usually a little phrase that says: "If there is any defect, return the merchandise to the manufacturer for a free replacement." The manufacturer is guaranteeing the potential of the thing.

God mercifully says to you, "If there are any defects, return to the Manufacturer." Isn't that a blessing? If you aren't working out, take your stuff back to the Chief. The Chief will work it out. "Come unto Me," God says. "I'm the only one who can fix you." God already has guaranteed what you can do.

You Can Do Everything God Asks

God is good. He has built into you the potential to produce everything He calls for. When God says, "Love your enemies," don't start listing reasons why you can't. The ability to love is built in...it's there...no excuses. God wouldn't ask for it if it wasn't available. He wired you to produce everything He demands.

God also wired everything else to produce what He demands from it. God looks at a piece of fruit and says, "In you there is a tree. There is a seed in you, and that seed is a tree. It's there, and I demand what I put in." So God says, "Plant that seed and a tree has to come out; I put a tree in that seed. Before you were given the fruit, I made the seed with the tree." That's the way God thinks. Hallelujah!

Whenever God gives you a responsibility, He also gives you the ability to meet that responsibility. In other words, *whatever God calls for, He provides for.* If God tells you to do something, He knows you can do it. So don't you dare tell God that you can't. Just because He told you to assume that responsibility means He knows you can do it. The problem isn't that you *can't*, it's just that you *won't*.

**Whenever God gives you a responsibility,
He also gives you the ability
to meet that responsibility.**

Whether you use the ability God has deposited within you is totally up to you. How well you assume the responsibilities God gives you is not so much a question of how much you *do*, but rather how much of the available power you *use*. What you are doing is not near what your ability is. What you have accomplished is a joke when compared with what you could accomplish—you are not working enough with the power of God (emphasis on work).

If You Think It, You Can Do It

You have a deposit of God's ability! Any person who sets a limit on what he *can* do, also sets a limit on what he *will* do. No one can determine how much you can produce except you and God. So there is nothing in this world that should stop you from accomplishing and realizing and fulfilling and maximizing your full potential.

Proverbs 23:7 tells us: If you can conceive it, you can do it. Obviously God is trying to communicate that you can *do* anything you can *think*. If you can conceive it, the fact that you can conceive it means you can do it. It doesn't matter if it's never been done—if you think it, you can do it. Likewise, if you never think it, you can't do it. God allows you to think only what you can do. If He doesn't allow you to think it, He knows you can't do it.

Think about the things you've been thinking recently. The fact that you thought them means you can do them. Now don't get me wrong. Thinking doesn't get it done. Thinking implies you can do it. See yourself doing the thing in your thoughts. Make your thought into an idea, and your idea into an imagination. Take that imagination and document it into a plan. Then go to it (of course with the proper rest periods). Put your plan into action. If you thought it, you can do it.

If God Has It, You Have It

But the fruit of the Spirit is love, joy, peace, patience, kindness, goodness, faithfulness, gentleness and self-control (Galatians 5:22-23).

Each of these fruits of the Spirit is an attribute of God. God unconditionally says, "They are you." God knows you have love. He knows you have joy—it doesn't matter what you are going through. God knows you have joy down there inside you, because Christ is joy.

Peace. How do you explain that? I used to think—the Prince of Peace. "Hello, Prince." I always thought: "Others have the peace. Give me some, Jesus." But that's not what the Bible teaches. The Bible says you *have* peace. When you are unhappy and everything is going wrong, God says, "Have peace." He doesn't say, "I'll give you some peace," because He can't give you what you already have. Peace is not a gift; it's a fruit. Joy is not a gift; it's a fruit. If God has it, you have it.

In the beginning there was only God. All that is and all that was, was in God—everything. We came out of God. Thus, everything that is in God, is in us: love...joy...peace...patience...kindness...goodness...faithfulness...gentleness...self-control. These are in God and in us.

"Love? I can't like that person."

"You're lying to me," God says. "What do you mean you can't love? Your spirit connected to My Spirit can do all things. Since I love, you can too."

As Romans 5:5 puts it: "...God has poured out His love into our hearts by the Holy Spirit..." After you return to God, the Holy Spirit brings love back to your heart. He ignites the stuff that has been in your heart all along. It's not that you *can't* love; you just don't *want* to love. Love isn't a decision you make, because you already have it. That's why you can love your enemies.

**Love isn't a decision you make,
because you already have it.
That's why you can love your enemies.**

Self-control. "Oh, Lord, I can't control myself." It's not that you can't, you won't. You have self-control—it's a fruit of the Spirit.

The last part of Galatians 5:23 says: "against such things there is no law [or limit]." There is not one of these things you can get too much of. You can't have too much patience, can you? You can never have too much love, can you? You are never too at peace. Peace cannot make you sick. Can you be too gentle or too kind? Can you ever be in so much control that you have too much self-control? These things are already in you, and God is saying, "Go for it!" You don't have to pray for these things. They are already in you if Christ is in you. Your potential is everything that is in Christ.

When you face difficulties, your answer is not in your pastor. Nor is it in your counselor or the books you read. These can be helpful for input, but the answer is in you. Christ in you—not in me. I have my own Christ image. You have yours. Christ in you the hope of glory.

Have Courage!

God walked up to a young man and gave him an assignment. The young man became scared because the assignment was very big. He didn't know if he could handle it. Joshua was so afraid he actually started to become visibly frightened at the prospect of the job. Do you know what God said to that young man? "Be courageous. I command you to be courageous." What challenge do you face? What are you afraid of? Just remember, fear is necessary for courage to exist. Courage can only be manifested in the presence of fear. So use fear to exercise your courage.

At first glance, that doesn't make any sense; because if Joshua was scared, he didn't have any courage. But God disagreed. The young man was commanded to display something he didn't know he had. When Joshua protested because Moses was going to turn the whole thing over to him, God said to Joshua, "Be strong and courageous" (Deuteronomy 31:7). He didn't say, "I'm going to give you strength." Nor did He say, "I'm going to give you courage." God just said, "Be still. Stop trembling. Stop talking negatively. Stop being afraid. Just be strong and courageous." God knew there was strength in Joshua. He knew the potential for courage was there. God simply called it out, deep calling unto deep: "Be strong. Be courageous."

Dominate the Earth

Then God said, "Let Us make man in Our image, in Our likeness, and let them rule over the fish of the sea and the birds of the air, over the livestock, over all the earth, and over all the creatures that move along the ground" (Genesis 1:26).

Your purpose for being is to dominate the earth. (God did not create you to go to church. You go to church because you need to relearn how to live again. Church is school, and when you graduate you will be dead. That's the perfect graduation ceremony—death. Then you finally will come back to who you really are.) You were created to dominate the earth. If God created you and commanded you to dominate the earth, God also is aware that you can do it.

God says, "Dominate the earth."

And you quickly reply, "But, but, but..."

Still God says, "Dominate the earth. I have created you to dominate the earth. I demand that you control, rule, govern, dominate, subdue and subject this planet."

God wouldn't have made that demand if you couldn't do it. He wired you to dominate this planet. You have the potential to dominate the earth because God placed within every human being the ability to dominate the planet. That is a very serious domination. You dare not complain when you are dominated by the earth (instead of the earth being dominated by you) because God has placed within you the capacity to do whatever He asks. Don't you dare tell God that you cannot do it. He did not give you the responsibility without also giving you the ability. He created you with the ability to dominate the earth.

You Are More Than You or Others Expect

One morning I said to my little boy as he ran into the room and jumped on me, "You know, I'm holding in my hands all you haven't been yet." Although he didn't understand much of what I was saying, I was thinking about the vast amount of potential that lay within him just waiting to be used. Potential is like that. It's all you can be and become that you haven't yet experienced. Think about it. Potential is all you are capable of being or doing or reaching. You haven't done it yet, but you can do it.

Thus when God tells you to dominate the earth, He is pointing to a potential that lies deep within you. Although it sounds simple to say that you have the potential to dominate the earth, that fact is a salvation to happiness. It is a blessing to know that God would never demand it if you couldn't do it. God has placed in you the ability to dominate the planet.

You Can Overcome Any Habit

You can overcome every habit, because God has clearly stated that you can. Isn't that amazing? That's a blessing! You are not involved in a hopeless fight. Oh, hear me if you are suffering a habit. The fact that God says "Do it!" is a joy. You can beat it.

Some of you have resolved that you are hooked for life. That's a lie. God gave you authority over that habit when He demanded that you rule the earth. Don't walk around with the hopeless idea: "I'll always be an addict. I'll always be an alcoholic. I'll always be like this."

God has placed within you the ability to dominate everything. It is there. It is in you. The problem isn't that you *can't* control your habit; the problem is that you *won't*.

People say: "I know I shouldn't be doing this." In reality that means: "I don't want to do this. Something is wrong with this but I can't help myself."

I have news for you—good news. It's more "I haven't decided to stop doing this," than "I shouldn't be doing this." You have what God demands. God will never demand anything He's not already provided for. Whatever God calls forth, He sees. God commanded you to dominate the earth, and the truth is you *can*.

**God will never demand anything
He's not already provided for.
Whatever God calls forth, He sees.**

Stop being ruled by cocaine or marijuana. Don't be the victim of alcohol and money. They are all but leaves from the trees that we are supposed to be dominating. Don't allow yourself to be at the beck and call of a little bottle that says: "Come here—come drink me." Don't allow yourself to be controlled by leaves from Colombia. The only way to escape these and other dominating habits is to understand your purpose for being. God did not create you to be dominated by sex or chemicals. He did not create you *to be controlled* by anything. He created you so *you could control* the earth.

You Are the Cream of the Crop

You are so much more than others expect from you. You are so much more than you expect from yourself. God calls us sanctified—that means special. God calls us elite—that means cream of the crop. And what God calls you He sees in you. God's not trying to conjure up things when He affirms who you are. He already sees them in you.

God looks under all the junk and says what He sees. He says: "You are pure. You are the righteousness of God in Christ Jesus." He looks beneath our unrighteous behavior and sees righteousness. He sees it and calls it out. He'll keep calling it out until it reaches the surface. God's not trying to *make you* into something. He's trying to expose the real you He already sees. While you are walking around trying to be good and righteous, God says, "You already are righteous."

**God's not trying to *make you*
into something. He's trying
to expose the real you He already sees.**

When you wake up tomorrow morning, stretch, look in the mirror and say: "You successful thing you." That's what God sees. No matter what kind of bum day is planned for you, you can decide in the morning that it's going to be a successful one. Why? Because this is the day the Lord has made. If you believe, it is possible the day will be good. It is possible to rejoice every day if you believe God has made it. Go ahead. Stretch. Look at the success that is just waiting to happen.

God Wants You to Know His Thoughts

When God told His people: "My thoughts are not your thoughts, neither are your ways My ways" (Isaiah 56:8), He was not saying He doesn't want our ways and thoughts to be like His. God was telling us: "Your thoughts and ways are not like Mine, but I'm trying to get them like Mine." God wants us to have a mind like His. He told us through the apostle Paul to be transformed by the renewing of our minds. He wants you to know and obey His will—doing what is pleasing and acceptable in His sight (Romans 12:2). Go back to the old mind in the garden. That's the way to think.

What a blessing it is to know that you can wake up tomorrow morning and have God's thoughts. But too often you wake up and say: "Oh, God. It's Monday."

God says: "You're not thinking like Me. This is a day I made just for you. Come on, let's go out there and give 'em heaven." Give 'em heaven? Yeah, that's right. There's a world out there that is hurting. Let's go give them heaven.

But we have the attitude: "Oh God. I can never be like You."

God comes to us and says, "My child, that's exactly what I want you to do. Have the mind of Christ. Think like Me." God wants you to adopt His mind and attitude toward yourself. He desires that you think about yourself the way He does. Believe His assessment of your potential.

Don't Let the World Determine Your Potential

We have allowed the world around us to determine our potential. Teachers say to students: "You are a C student."

The student then goes around believing that, and he becomes an average student for the rest of his life—an average person even. He becomes an average husband. She becomes an average wife. We become average parents and average children with average attitudes and IQs. And when we turn out to be average, our parents say: "Well, honey, you have my genes." No. They received your attitude that was transmitted to you from that teacher.

You need to shake off what people call IQs. Do you know what "IQ" means? It means Intelligent Quotient—it's what people believe your degree of intelligence is based upon some tests you take. These tests measure your motor skills, your thinking ability, your cognitive ability, your reading ability, your math ability, etc. Then based on these tests they say, "You are a D student. You are a D person." You haven't even grown up yet and they are telling you what you are going to be and do! They don't know what you are going to do.

Unfortunately, people believe what they are told based on those tests. There are thousands of examples in history of men and women who were put off and cast out as misfits. Later they turned out to be some of the world's greatest leaders. We must be careful when we start putting Intelligent Quotients on people. Your potential has nothing to do with those tests. Only God determines your potential. Your IQ is spelled *H-O-L-Y S-P-I-R-I-T*. Your IQ is something that goes far beyond the pages of a test. It goes all the way to God.

Spirits Cannot Die

One day as I was talking with the Holy Spirit, He said to me, "Myles, what are you?"

I said, "Spirit."

He said, "Yea! You got that down! Do you know that spirits cannot die?"

I said, "This is true."

Then He said, "Why do humans think in terms of time only? I came back to earth to introduce humans to eternity."

I said, "Whoa!"

Then the Holy Spirit showed me how God had designed us to live forever. He said, "If you have to live forever, which you will, what are you going to do? God intended you to live forever because spirits never die. And you have to live forever being fulfilled. God never makes anything without a purpose. So you are designed to live forever and you've got to be fulfilling your purpose in life. God had to make sure He stored enough in you to last forever so you will never get bored."

That blew my mind. We are going to live forever.

Sometimes we sing: "When I get to heaven I'm going to praise the Lord for a thousand years."

"What are you going to do after that?"

"Well, then I'll walk around the streets of gold for another thousand years."

"What are you going to do after that?" You have eternity to live. After a million years of worshipping and bowing and keeping company with the angels, what are you going to do? Your mind is so small. You think, "Wow. Look what I have accomplished."

God says, "Gosh, your life is a spot in eternity—just a drop in eternity. You will not begin really living until you leave time and enter eternity."

God has packed so much into you that the book He wrote on you is only the book for time. Your potential from birth to death is contained in that book—a book so full of expectations that David says it is vast.

Only a Page

I recently attended a function to honor a gentleman in our community—a tremendous man. Several people gave speeches about him, talking about his many accomplishments. As I sat there I thought, "Wow! If you only knew."

A booklet on the table listed all the things he had accomplished. As I looked at it I thought, "Is that all—half a page?" There's a book on that man and he only has a page.

Created for Eternal Life

From eternity, God has been our dwelling place. Before there was anything, we were in God. Before the mountains were born or the world was created, God existed. God was pregnant with everything, including us. We always have been. In the former state we were unseen, but we still existed. We are not haphazard. We didn't come here by mistake. From before the beginning, we were in God.

God is called a creator because He always has something to do. God is always busy doing something. When God took us out of Himself, He gave us part of His Spirit. God is Spirit and spirits are eternal. They cannot die. Therefore, what is spirit and comes out of God is also eternal. I believe one of God's greatest success projects is me—and you. When God created human beings, He said, "This one will keep Us excited forever. Let's make and create a being in Our own image. Let's make one who will not fade away." Mountains will fade away and rivers will run dry. Streams will evaporate and the oceans will go away. But when God came up with man, He created something that would last forever. He took man out of Himself. God made you spirit and put so much stuff in you that it will take an eternal life to live it all. *Your true potential requires eternal life to be realized and maximized.*

There's No Retirement in the Bible

There are times when we get tired of our jobs. In fact, we get so tired that we look for retirement. And when we get it, we just want to retire—we want to stop permanently. God says to us: "You have it all wrong. Your thinking is wrong. There is no retirement in the Bible. It is not in My thinking." God doesn't think retirement. The only thing God thinks is rest. Why? Because God knows you have eternity to go just like He does. God wants you to assist Him in creating and developing and dominating and ruling forever and ever and ever. That's a long time. The wealth of your potential is so rich it requires an eternal life to bring it out.

We are not going to be in heaven for a million years bowing down around a throne. God doesn't have an ego problem. He doesn't need us to tell Him how nice He is. In fact, He was nice without us. We make Him look pretty bad. We've really messed up God. We came out of God. We are the only ones made in His image, and look what we did. God was better off without us. He doesn't need our praises to make Him feel high.

Now don't get me wrong. I'm not talking down heaven. I'm trying to open your mind. God has so much in store for you that He said, "No eye has seen, no ear has heard, no mind has conceived what God has prepared for those who love Him" (1 Corinthians 2:9). The Holy Spirit will continue to unfold it and reveal it until eternity ends—which it won't. God has placed enough potential in you to last forever. Try to do as much now as you can. Pack as much as you can into the 70 to 100 years you have here. Go for it. Go for a hunk of gold. Go for the mountain that has the gold in it. Go for the whole thing. Because if you can think it, you can do it. God is the limit of your ability. He won't allow you to think it if you can't do it.

PRINCIPLES

---

1. The potential of a thing is related to its source.

2. Your potential is as great as God's potential, because when God wanted you He spoke to Himself.

3. Potential is determined by the demands made on it by the creator.

4. If you can think it, you can do it.

5. Your potential is everything that is in Christ. So if God has it, you have it.

6. God created you and commanded you to dominate the earth.

7. God will never demand anything He hasn't already provided for. Whatever God calls forth, He sees.

8. The wealth of your potential is so rich it requires an eternal life to bring it out.

8 | Challenge Your Ability

Your ability needs responsibility to expose its possibilities. Do what you can with what you have where you are.

Theodore Roosevelt

The people who are blessings to humanity are usually men and women who decide there is more to them than what other people have said. People who bless the world are people who believe there is an ability inside them to accomplish something that has never been done. Though they may not know *exactly* what they can do, they *try* because they believe they can accomplish something.

How High Can You Jump?

I remember the day I found out that I can jump real high—about eight feet high. Now, I can't jump that high intentionally, but I did it once when I was a little boy.

There was a lady who lived behind our house from whose fruit trees we would occasionally feast and help ourselves. When we were little kids, we would crawl under the fence. One day while I was on her side of the fence, her very vicious dog suddenly appeared. I had just touched down after climbing the fruit tree. As I carefully considered the distance between the fence, the dog and myself, I knew I had to make a run for it. I ran toward the fence with the dog close behind me. As the fence came closer and closer, all I could say was "O God, I'm dead." All I could think was "jump." As I left the ground, my heart was pounding and my chest felt like an arcade full of shouting people. I was so afraid! When I landed, I was safely on the other side of the fence.

When I turned around and looked at the dog, he was barking angrily because he couldn't get over the fence. I just thought, "Yea, good for you." Suddenly I became very proud because I had gotten away from him. But when I started to realize what I had done, I looked at the fence and thought, "How did I do that?"

I thank God for that dog. He was a blessing in my life. I never jumped that high before, and I never have since, but at least I know that I did it. I discovered that day there is a lot more potential in me than I realized was there.

The same is true for you. You aren't doing more because no one has challenged you. I want to take you from the realm of waiting for people to challenge you and encourage you to challenge yourself. Don't wait for a dog to teach you how to jump. Jump by your own challenge. Don't just look at life and say, "Well, I'm going to wait until a demand is made on me and then I will produce." Make a demand on yourself. Say to yourself, "Look, I am going to become the best in this area no matter what people have done before me." Then go after that. You will accomplish it if you set out to do it.

Tell Me to Come

That reminds me of a young fisherman who decided, "I'm going to take a chance and try to walk on water." One night as the disciples were crossing Lake Galilee it was hard rowing. They were being tossed about by the waves because the wind was against them. As they struggled, a man came toward them, walking on the water. In fear they cried out, "It's a ghost." Only when He spoke to them did the disciples recognize that it was Jesus. Peter then said, "Lord, if it's you...tell me to come to you on the water" (Matthew 14:28). And when Jesus said *"Come!"*, Peter had the guts to respond to Jesus' order.

I believe every one of those disciples could have walked on water. The potential was in them even as it was in Peter. But only Peter succeeded, because only Peter had the guts to say, "If you challenge me, I'll take your challenge." Although we may laugh or criticize Peter for sinking, none of us has ever walked on water. He's the only guy who can say in heaven when we get there, "I walked on water. What did you do?"

Everybody sees Jesus, but very few of us ask Jesus, "Tell me something to do. Give me something to challenge my potential." Men and women who are assets to the world and bring change for the better are those who give their potential something to maximize. *Give your ability a responsibility,* that would change the world. There is a wealth of ability in you, but you haven't given it any responsibility. Don't die without maximizing your ability—that's irresponsible. You have no right to die with what God put in you to live out.

Don't Wait to Be Challenged

God has promised that He can do far more than you can think or imagine. His power is available to you. Is that power working in you? Are you saying to God: "I've got some power, now work it for me. Give me something to do"?

God has given you a skill or ability the world needs. He has been waiting for your birth. Perhaps He planted within you a unique ability to work for life. Imagine a dead baby turning purple in your hand. Others are thinking "undertaker," but you know that God has given you a potential to restore life. You believe God and pray, by the power of His Spirit, "God, this dear baby must live." Even though some-one might overhear you, and that makes your prayer all the more difficult, you tap into the potential God planted deep within you and believe for the baby's life.

God has given you a skill or ability the world needs.

Miracles happen when we give our potential respon-sibility. God designed it that way. Don't allow the things within you to die with you because you did not challenge them. God planted the seed of potential within you. He made you according to the *potential principle*—like the rest of His creation. Don't waste that gift. Give your potential some responsibility.

Beat the Odds

Men and women who make changes in history are those who have come against the odds and told the odds it is impossible for the odds to stop them. Don't throw yourself away—don't let anyone else throw you away—because you are up against some odds.

The minute we see somebody in a wheelchair something happens to us. We think the person is half a person. We almost treat him as if we apologize for his condition. We look at people who are blind...who have a withered hand... who walk with a limp...who have only one arm as though they are half a person. We limit their potential to the wheel-chair or the limp or the missing hand or the short arm. We reduce everybody to their bodies. You are not your body. Some of the greatest minds in the world are in wheelchairs.

I think about President Roosevelt in a wheelchair. Did you ever think an invalid could be the president of one of the greatest nations on earth? I think of a young boy I recently read about. A great mathematician, he's suffering from a disease that destroys his bones. He's just sort of fading away. You should see him. He looks ugly compared to what we call beauty. His glasses are falling off on the side because his face is falling in. His nose is almost gone. His teeth are all messed up. His whole body is warped. He can't write. But they say he has the greatest mathematical calculations of our day. Professors come to his home, sit at his desk, and write everything he says. They are developing mathematical books for the universities from this brain in the chair. His illness has not destroyed his potential. His genius is not affected by his physical appearance. He's a young man who is beating the odds by using all the formulas God stored within him.

Suppose you end up in a wheelchair next year with all the brains you have right now. Will you quit? Is your dream related to your body? Don't say "no" too fast. Some of you would just quit and get totally depressed and so sad. You'd say, "Oh, life didn't work out for me," and you'd allow all the dreams you have right now to die in the chair. You'd simply quit.

**Suppose you end up in a wheelchair
next year with all the brains
you have right now. Will you quit?**

I think about Mr. Penney who started J. C. Penneys. Born an orphan with no mother and no father (he didn't even know who his parents were), he refused to be like many people I know who sit around and say: "Everybody treats me bad. No one cares for me. I guess I ought to go on drugs and just blow it." Penney decided that there was a food store in him and a clothing store and a department store. So he acquired his first job working in a store packing bags. I can almost hear him saying in his mind as he packed bags one day: "One of these days they're going to pack these for me." Like many others who have given much to mankind, Penney believed that he had the ability to make something of his life. And now we go and spend our credit card money at his J. C. Penney stores.

Don't give up because you are physically handicapped. Don't give up if you are facing great odds. Your potential is not determined by whether you can see the fine print of a book, walk across the street or lift heavy objects with both hands. Your potential is not destroyed because your mother is an alcoholic, your father's a junkie or you have no parents at all. There are many people in wheelchairs who have given up. There are many people who come from the wrong side of town or a bad family situation who have given up. Don't be one of them. Beat the odds.

Shortcuts Don't Work

Ben Johnson is an athlete from Canada who set many world records. In 1987 he set the world record in the one hundred yard dash at 9.83 seconds. In 1988 he broke his own record, winning the race in 9.79. But it is difficult to be correct in calling that a world record because the last record set was not the record of Ben Johnson. It was the record of a steroid pill. That record belongs to Ben Johnson plus the chemicals.

We will never know Ben Johnson's potential as far as running the one hundred yard dash is concerned. Could he have run one hundred yards in 9.79 seconds without the chemical? Possibly, but we will never know because Ben Johnson negated his potential by trying a shortcut. There was no reason for his shortcut. He had a world record. He had his name in history, and it was a good name. How sad to destroy a good name by a little bit of chemical.

I picked up a magazine on an airplane in which there was an advertisement that said, "Would you like a doctorate degree? Call us." I often read that advertisement and wonder how many have called them. If I did not realize that you cannot get something for nothing, I probably would have called them. Many have. There are people out there with doctorate degrees, or with doctorate letters in front of their names, who will never know their potential. They didn't allow themselves the chance to see what they could really do. They have the degrees, but they didn't fulfill the requirements.

There are no shortcuts to developing your potential. You will never know what you might have achieved if you use a crutch to get there. You'll never know what you may have learned if you get a degree without fulfilling the require-ments. You will never know what you can do if you attempt to obtain it by a shortcut. Shortcuts negate potential. They destroy the possibilities God planted within you.

Demand Something of Your Potential

After God created Adam, He gave him a job. God knew Adam's potential to name all the animals would never be released unless it was challenged. Potential must be exercised to be fulfilled. Demands must be made on potential if it is to be release and fulfilled. God has given you potential. Un-less you make demands on it, you will die with it. Unless you venture to try things you've never done before, you'll never experience the wealth that lives within you. Decide today, "I'm going to do something I've never done before." "I'm going to get a promotion this year in my job." "I'm going to win more people to Jesus this year than my church and my pastor ever did." If you have a business, resolve to cut the overhead and increase service. Give your potential some demands. It needs to be maximized and challenged.

Potential must be exercised to be fulfilled.

The greatest works in the world will be done by people who don't care who gets the credit. I don't want to be famous, I just want to be faithful. I don't want to be well-known, I want to be well-used. I don't want to be powerful, I want to be potent. Success requires striking out on new paths instead of traveling those that are well-worn. Genius is one percent inspiration and ninety-nine percent perspiration. There are many people with great ideas, but they have no desire to try. There are four steps to the accomplishment of your dream: Prepare prayerfully. Plan purposefully. Proceed positively. Pursue persistently. Failure is the path of least persistence.

Don't Be Afraid to Try

No one can climb beyond the limitations he has placed on himself. Success is never final—failure is never fatal. It is courage that counts—courage and the willingness to move on. A great deal of talent is lost to the world for want of a little courage. Every day sends to the grave, obscure men, whom fear and timidity have prevented from making their first attempt to do something. Never tell a person that something can't be done, because God may have been waiting for centuries for someone ignorant enough to believe that the impossible could be possible.

**Success is never final—
failure is never fatal.**

The poorest of men are men without a dream. Don't be so afraid of failure that you refuse to try. Demand something of yourself. Failure is only an incident. There's more than the failure—there's success deep behind that failure. Failure is the opportunity to more intelligently begin again. When you fail, that is a great chance to start again. Learn from it and move on. Don't be paralyzed by the failure.

One good thing about failure is that it is proof that you tried. The greatest mistake you can make is to be afraid of making one. People who do nothing in life are usually people who do nothing. People who don't make mistakes in life are usually people who didn't have a chance to make any because they never tried. Challenge your potential. Demand things of yourself that are beyond what you have already done. Expect more from yourself than the accomplishments that are easily within your reach. What you have is not all you are. The limit of your potential is God. It is better to attempt a thing and fail, than to never try and not know you could succeed.

PRINCIPLES

---

1. Believe there is potential in you to accomplish something worthwhile.

2. Unless you use your potential, you will never realize how much ability is inside you.

3. Jump by your own challenge. Don't wait for someone to challenge you.

4. Don't let the odds that are against you stop you from fulfilling your potential.

5. Shortcuts negate your ability.

6. Don't be so afraid of failure that you refuse to try.

9 | The Key to Your Potential

The secret to a happy and productive life is remaining attached to your Source.

A grape vine is an interesting plant. The vine, which is the thick wooden part running from the ground up the pole, is the only part of the plant that contains life ability. None of the life is in the branches; all of it is in the vine. There is no life in the little green things you see on the side with the grapes hanging on them. They are getting their life from the vine. They have no root in themselves. If you were to break one of those green branches off and plant it in the ground, it would never grow because it has no life ability in it. Each small branch has to depend on the life flowing up and down the great branch, the vine, to give it life. Thus the branches cannot live without the vine. The relationship of the vine and its branches is reflected throughout God's creation. Life is not possible when a thing is separated from its source.

All Things Have a Source

When God created the world, He first decided what He wanted His creation to be made out of. Then He spoke to that source, and whatever God said came out of what He spoke to. Whenever God wants to create something, He first decides what He wants the thing to be made out of. Then He speak to whatever He wants it made out of, and whatever God speaks comes out of what He spoke to.

When God wanted plants He spoke to the soil, and out of the soil came what God spoke. Since God wanted plants to be made out of soil, every plant is dirt. When God wanted animals He spoke to the ground. Because animals came out of the ground, they are one hundred percent dirt. The principle is simple. Whatever God wants He speaks to what He wants it made out of. Whatever God speaks comes out of what He spoke to.

Whatever God speaks comes out of what He spoke to.

When God wanted animals He spoke to the ground. When God wanted plants He spoke to dirt. Because God wanted man to come out of Himself, He spoke to Himself when He created man.

> Then God said, "Let Us make man in Our image, in Our likeness, and let them rule over...all the creatures that move along the ground." So God created man in His own image; in the image of God He created him; male and female He created them (Genesis 1:26-27).

When God wanted man, He spoke to Himself. Therefore man is what God spoke to. Man is spirit because man came out of the spirit realm.

Source Determines Potential

Everything God creates has the same components as its source. Wherever something comes from determines it components. Or to say it another way: Everything is made up of the same stuff as what it came out of. Therefore plants are made up of one hundred percent dirt. They consist of the same things as the dirt. Animals also are one hundred percent dirt, or whatever is in the soil.

**Everything is made up of the same stuff
as what it came out of.**

So when a plant dies, it goes back to where it came from—you can't find it. When an animal dies, it goes back to where it came from—you can't find it. When man dies, he goes back to the spirit realm.

So whatever something comes from determines the components of which it is made. And whatever something comes from determines its potential. *Potential is related to source.* A plant can be no more than the dirt can be. Likewise, animals can be no more than the dirt can be. Since you came out of God, you have the same components as God and your potential is determined by God.

Life Is Maintained by Its Source

Wherever something comes from, it has to remain attached to where it came from in order to fulfill itself. All created things must be maintained by their source. Thus plants need soil to live. They can't live without the dirt. If a plant decides, "I'm tired of the soil," it also decides "I'm ready to die." Animals also need the dirt. Because they must live on what they came from, they have to eat plants and one another (dirt) to stay alive. If an animal decides, "I'm not going to eat anymore dirt or anything that is made from the dirt," he has decided to die. Therefore, if you decide you don't need God, you have also decided never to become all you are capable of being. The potential of everything is related to source; everything must be attached to its source if it is going to fulfill its potential.

If you decide you don't need God, you also have decided never to become all you are capable of being.

Like the branches of the grape vine, our life depends upon our Source. When God wanted human beings, He spoke to Himself—God is our Source. We came out of God and contain a measure of His ability. But our only hope of fulfilling that ability lies in God. We must be hooked up with God if we are going to tap any of our true potential. Jesus came to bring us back to God so God's original intention when He took man out of Himself could be fulfilled. Thus the key to your full potential is staying related to God.

I Am the True Vine

As a plant cannot fulfill its potential without being in relationship with the soil, so you cannot fulfill your true potential without being related to God. Thus Jesus says in the fifteenth chapter of John: "I am the true vine" (John 15:1). Jesus calls Himself the *true vine* because there are a lot of other vines around to get hooked into: education, philosophy, science, even religion.

The word *vine* here literally means "source of life." Like the grape vine for its branches, Jesus is our Source of life. If you depend on education, all you are going to have is what education can offer—an intellectual stimulation. No matter how many degrees you get, you are living below your potential because you are feeding on a false vine. You will never know your true information capacity if you are stuck on education. There are people who have been out of school for fifty years who don't know any more now than they knew when they were in school. Jesus says, "I am the True Vine." By this statement He implies that there are vines or sources that are not genuine.

Pruning for Potential

The potential of the branches and the vine needs the attention of the gardener. The gardener works in the vineyard trying to bring as much life as possible out of the vines. Often he prunes the vines because he knows there is more life down in the roots. Since he is aware that he isn't getting the full capacity of the vine, he begins to clip some of the branches. Cutting off the old leaves that stop the vine from producing its full potential, the gardener starts to clean up the vine.

In Scripture, God is described as our gardener. Like the gardener in the vineyard, the Father comes into your life and starts clipping at the habits that are hanging on and the attitudes that are killing you. He trims a little bit here and a little bit there from the bad relationships that are stunting your potential and restricting your growth. The Gardener says, "You can do better than you are doing." *Clip*. "Stop lying." *Clip*. "Stop disobeying me." *Clip*. Carefully and steadily, God cuts off those things that are holding you back, because He knows you are not living up to your possibilities. He knows you're not measuring up to the Source from which you came. The ability of the One to whom you are hooked up is much greater than you are displaying. There is more in your roots.

You're not measuring up to the Source from which you came.

Are there some old leaves in your life that have been hanging around for five, ten or fifteen years? Do you need to quit a habit or two so your life more truly reflects the potential of the One who made you? Are you wasting time planning, setting up, committing and feeling guilty about sin? How many hours in a day are you losing to disobedience and rebellion? Prune your life through discipline and obedience to God, who desires your potential to be maximized. Remember, all God's commands and laws are given to maximize your performance and free your potential.

Freed to Obey

When God placed Adam and Eve in the garden of Eden, He said, "You are free to eat from any tree in the garden; but you must not eat from the tree of the knowledge of good and evil, for when you eat of it you will surely die" (Genesis 2:16). God gives you freedom, but He also puts some limitations on you. Whenever you violate your limitations, you are in rebellion against God. The only limitations of your potential are violations of God's Word. If you do anything that doesn't violate the Word of God, you are within your freedom. God gives you freedom to do anything except disobey Him. That's a tremendous freedom. You are free to do anything within the context of God's Word. If God says it's cool, go for it, because the possibilities of your life are all connected with God.

God gives you freedom to do anything except disobey Him.

God comes into your life with pruning shearers to free you from your disobedience and rebellion. He comes to take out those things that are stopping you from developing and growing and obeying. Imagine how different your life might have been if you had not wasted months or years on a particular habit. Imagine how different your life could be if you would let go of a grudge or clean up your language. Anything that is contrary to the Word of God is subject to God's pruning. He comes into your life to help you clean up your act. He wants you to enjoy the freedom of obedience and life within His limitations. Bearing a pruning shear, God trims the useless and dead wood from your life so you can draw from Him the fresh fulness of your potential.

Then Jesus says, "Okay, you're clean. I've saved you. You're hooked up, straightened out and fixed. You know who your Source is and your pipe's been unclogged. Your holes have been mended and you're ready to flow. Now stay that way by remaining hooked up to Me." You are cleansed through the word Jesus speaks to you when you ask Him to forgive you. The lid on your well, put there through your disobedience and satan's deception, has been pried off. You are clean and free to do *anything* that doesn't violate God's Word—free to be all you were created to be and do (whatever He says you can do). What freedom!—freedom that can last, so long as you remain hooked up to God. The Son is Life and the Father is the Maximizer.

Prerequisite for Potential

Living a victorious life does not depend on us. It depends on who we are hooked up to. Jesus said,

> Remain in Me, and I will remain in you. No branch can bear fruit by itself; it must remain in the vine. Neither can you bear fruit unless you remain in Me (John 15:4).

There are many individuals who I expected to be successful in life—their lives showed tremendous potential—but they lost their relationship with their Source. Jesus says, "If you abide in Me, you will be fruitful. But you cannot do it on your own." No branch can live by itself; it must remain attached to the vine. Neither can it bear fruit apart from the vine. Jesus is the true vine. You are a branch. If you remain in Christ and Christ in you, you will bear abundant fruit. If you do not remain in Christ, you are like a branch that whithers and is thrown away. No branch can bear fruit if it is not attached. It starts going in the opposite direction. No matter how talented or gifted you are, you will never be truly fulfilled and successful apart from a personal relationship with your Creator-Source.

> **If you remain in Me and My words remain in you, ask whatever you wish and it will be given you** (John 15:7).

Jesus' words are almost frightening—whatever you wish. God will give you whatever you ask for so long as you remain in Him. What a promise! When you open your life completely to God, the Holy Spirit's crowbar firmly resists satan's attempt to recap your well. The wealth of your potential becomes limitless and free. Whatever you imagine will be done, because God won't allow you to think it unless you can do it.

Thus the secret to a happy, productive life is remaining attached to your Divine Source. If you abide in Christ, His word will abide in you. You can ask whatever you wish and it will be given to you. God will provide from the depths of His grace...freely, abundantly, victoriously. You don't have to hustle. You don't have to plead. God is always waiting to help you live a full, fruitful, complete life. From His storehouse of riches, God will supply all you can imagine, and more because *He wants you to fulfill your potential.* So long as you remain attached to the Vine and submitted to the discipline of the Gardener, you will know God's blessings. Your potential requires a relationship with its Source.

God created you to exalt and bring glory to His name. When you bear fruit, God is glorified. His name is exalted whenever you use the abilities He stored in you. The whole purpose for your being—to reflect and increase the glory of God—is fulfilled whenever you maximize your potential.

God works hard to keep us hooked up with Him. He wants His glory to fill the earth through us.

For Disciples Only

What kind of life are you living? Are you in tune with Christ or are you off doing your own thing? Is there sin clogging up your pipes, preventing you from accomplishing and achieving your maximum ability? Are you constantly hustling, struggling to make your way in the world? If you are, you probably have not become a disciple of the Risen Christ. You see, being a Christian is not enough to fulfill your potential. The word "Christian" was given to us by pagans. Jesus never called us "Christians." This term was given to the disciples in the early Church by the pagans in Antioch.

The Bible calls us "children of God" and "citizens of the Kingdom." We are God's offspring, a people who have been reconnected to their Source. Only disciples, those who are committed to abiding in Christ, will maximize their potential. A disciple is a learner who follows a teacher everywhere he goes. His goal is to learn and keep on learning until he resembles the teacher. Only a disciple experiences full potential. Because his greatest desire is to know and resemble the Master, he spends hours listening to His words. He seeks new visions, revelations and understandings concerning the Master's life and who He calls His disciples to be.

Only a disciple experiences full potential.

I do not consider myself to be great or superior to anyone else, but I decided at the age of fourteen that I wanted to understand everything that God has prepared for me. I invested hours in the Word of God—large chunks... sometimes half a day. After 15 years, God said to me, "That's still not enough. Follow me." Over the years He has blessed me with a greater degree of understanding and wisdom from His Word. He's given me revelations of His life, and visions of who He is and who I am and should be. I don't want to stop. I'm not great, but I want to be one of the few. I want you to be one of the few. I'll lay down my life to have you be one of the few. Don't fall for the limitations of the world—the lies and deceptions of the lower nature. Find your Source and get connected. Then stay connected. God has chosen you to go and bear fruit—fruit that will last. Abide in Christ, and the Father will give you whatever you wish. Refuse to live below your privileged potential. Reach for the fruit that are still within the branches of your life. Drink deep from the vine and let your life feed others.

PRINCIPLES

---

1. What God speaks to is the source for what He creates.

2. Everything has the same components as its source.

3. Nothing can live without being attached to its source.

4. Jesus is your Source of life.

5. God prunes your life to bring you into the freedom of obedience.

6. The key to fulfilling your potential is staying hooked up to God.

7. Only disciples—those who are committed to abiding in Christ—will maximize their potential.

8. God is glorified when you use your abilities.

10 | Limiting Your Unlimited Potential

The potency of your potential requires eternal life to be realized.

As we discuss the awesome task of tapping our true and full potential, it is essential that we come to appreciate how important each one of us is and how special we are to God. If you were aware of how much power and worth you have, the first thing that would be affected would be your attitude toward yourself.

Many of us have a difficult time projecting a good attitude toward others because we feel bad about ourselves. Great positive thinkers and personal motivators, along with psychologists, all agree that if you feel good about yourself, then your attitude toward others will be influenced by that attitude. However, for many positive thinking programs, this is simply an attempt to convince one's self by mental assent that you are of value and worth. It's an attempt to convince you of something you don't believe.

On the contrary, what we are discussing here is something different. We are talking here about a fact grounded in truth and reality, and established by the One who created you. Your worth, value and potential have all been given by

God, and there is no formula, test or scheme to measure the full extent of these qualities and abilities. Therefore I would like to reiterate some principles and concepts that were discussed in earlier chapters. It is essential that you understand these if you are going to tap into your true and full potential.

Potential Unlimited

A principle discussed in chapter two states: *Everything that is was in God.* In essence, everything that exists came out of God or proceeded out of His creative Spirit. He is the Source of everything. The first verse of the book of Genesis introduces God as the Creator of all things...

In the beginning God created the heavens and the earth (Genesis 1:1).

But I would again like to take you back before time began, before there was a creation. Let's consider what I call the verse before Genesis 1:1. We'll call it Genesis 1:0. Where was everything before creation came to be? I suggested that the first verse of the Bible could be written as follows:

Before there was a beginning, there was God. Before there was a creation, there was a Creator. Before anything was, there was God (Genesis 1:0).

The above verse means God did not begin when the beginning began—He began the beginning. He did not start when start got started—He started start. There was no beginning without God. He is the Source, Creator and Sustainer of everything. Nothing exists that He did not create. If it does not exist, it is because He has not yet created it. He is the ultimate Source of everything. Anything and everything that comes after the beginning has to come out of God.

In the beginning was the Word, and the Word was with God, and the Word was God. He was with God in the

beginning. Through Him all things were made; without Him nothing was made that has been made (John 1:1-2).

Before anything existed, God had it in Him. That is the reason we ascribe to God only the term *omni-potent*. *Potent* is the word from which we derive the word *potential*. *Omni* is defined as meaning *all* or *everything*. Therefore the ascription *omnipotent* means *one who is* all potential *or* all power—all ability, *seen or unseen, used or unused, manifested or yet unmanifested*. God does not only *have* potential; He *is* potential—and the Source of all potential. The source of all potential is in the Omnipotent One.

PRINCIPLE: The potential of a thing is related to its source.

The source of all potential is in the Omnipotent One.

This means wherever something comes from determines the potential it has. The degree or potency of that potential can be measured by the demands made on it by the one who made it. Therefore, the potential or ability of a thing is determined by the purpose for which the creator, manufacturer or maker made it. Every product is designed and engineered by the manufacturer to fulfill its purpose. Therefore its potential is built in. The purpose establishes the demands to be placed on the product, and the demands determine its potential.

This principle is evidenced by all manufacturers who enclose a *manual* with their product detailing the expected performance and potential of their product. The manufacturer wants you to read the manual before using the product so it can tell you what demands to make on the product. They are confident you can make those demands because they have already built into the product the necessary components to fulfill the demands. The potential of a thing is therefore not determined by opinions, assumptions or prejudices, but only by the demands placed on it by the one who made it.

Your true ability and potential should not be measured by the limitations of an academic test or an Intelligence Quotient score. Nor should it be determined by the social, cultural, economic and educational "norms" of your society. Society did not create you. You are not a product of your culture. You are not the offspring of your economy. You were not created by the Department of Education. Therefore, none of these has the right to determine how much potential you really possess. If you want to know how much potential you have, first discover who created or manufactured you. Then check the demands He is making upon your life. Whatever He is demanding of you, *you can do.*

> **PRINCIPLE: The potential of a thing is determined by the demands made on it by the one who made it.**

What Are the Limits of Your Potential?

It seems to me that the people who change the world and significantly impact humanity are those who have discovered the limitless nature of their potential. They are people who decided to take the word *impossible* out of their dictionaries. If you are going to realize and maximize your full potential, you will have to understand the true nature of your potential. But to do this, you must first understand the process of your creation and the Source from which you came. At this point, I wish to review a principle we shared earlier that is essential to understanding this process.

When God created the earth and made the fullness of its beauty, He used the following principle:

1. He purposed and decided what He wanted;

2. He then decided what kind of material substance He wanted it made from;

3. He then spoke to the substance or material from which He wanted it made;

4. And whatever He said to what He was speaking to came out of what He spoke to—exactly what He said.

5. Whatever came out of what God spoke to was made of the same material substance from which it came.

In essence, whatever God spoke to became the same material for the thing that came out of what He spoke it from. This process-principle is evidenced in the first chapter of Genesis. For example, when God wanted to create plant life and vegetation, He said:

"Let the land [dirt, soil] **produce vegetation: seed-bearing plants and trees..." And it was so. The land produced vegetation...** (Genesis 1:11-12)

When God wanted to make stars, He said:

"Let there be lights in the expanse of the sky [the firmament of the heavens—the gasses in space] **to separate the day from the night..." And it was so** (Genesis 1:14-15).

When God wanted fish or marine life, He said:

"Let the waters [or the soil under the water] **teem with living creatures..." So God created the great creatures of the sea and every living and moving thing with which the water teems...** (Genesis 1:20-21)

When God wanted animals, He said:

"Let the land [soil, dirt] **produce living creatures..." And it was so. So God made...all the creatures that move along the ground...** (Genesis 1:24-25)

If you examine these scriptures from Genesis, you will discover: Whatever God wanted He spoke to the material substance from which He wanted it made. He wanted plants to be made out of soil or dirt, so He spoke them out of the earth. That is why, when a plant dies, it decomposes back to the soil. He spoke the stars from the gasses in space; therefore stars are one hundred percent high density nuclear gas explosions. When a star "dies," it dissipates into gasses and returns to its original state. (Scientists have recently discovered this to be true.) Because God wanted animals made from the soil (dirt), God spoke to the earth when He created them. Animals are therefore one hundred percent soil (dirt). When animals die, they too decompose and return to the soil. The same process and principle is also true of marine life.

Therefore, when God wanted plants and vegetation, He spoke to the soil. When He wanted stars, He spoke to the gasses. When He wanted fish, He spoke to the water. And when He wanted animals, He spoke to the earth. *But when God wanted you (man), He spoke to* Himself. It is important to understand here that whatever God speaks to produces what God says and is therefore composed of the same material substance. So as plants are soil, stars are gasses and animals are soil (dirt), even so *man is spirit, because he came out of God.* Man does not *have* a spirit, he *is* spirit—because of the Source from which he came.

Man does not *have* a spirit, he *is* spirit— because of the Source from which he came.

This process-principle of creation also introduces us to additional principles that we must understand if we are to fully appreciate the nature of our potential. These principles are evidenced in nature and are scientifically sound. They are as follows:

1. **Whatever God wants He speaks to what He wants it made out of.**

2. **Wherever something came from, it is composed of the same material substance as where it came from. It is a composite of its source.**

3. **Wherever something came from, it has to be sustained and maintained by where it came from.**

4. **The potential of a thing cannot be fulfilled without being related to its source.**

These principles are clearly demonstrated by God's system of creation in nature. The plants came from the earth and they *must* remain related (attached) to the earth in order to live and be fruitful. The stars came from the gasses in space and *must* therefore remain in space in order to remain effective. The fish came from the water and *must* remain related (submerged) in water in order to live. The animals are products of the soil from which God spoke them and *must* remain related (feed on) soil (dirt) products in order to live. This holds true for man also: Man (spirit) came out of God (source) and must remain related (attached) to God (his source) in order to live.

Man came out of God and must remain related to God in order to live.

As the plants need dirt and the fish need water, *so man needs God.* If man is to realize and maximize his true potential, a relationship with God is not an option. It is a necessity. If man is to become all he was purposed to be, God is not an alternative for man, but a requirement.

This point is crucial because it helps us understand the ultimatums of Jesus and the emphatic demands of God the Father. The call of the Kingdom is not that we *should* be born of the *spirit,* but that we *must* be born of the *spirit.* Jesus didn't say, "I am *a way,*" but "I am *the way*" (John 14:6). It was also He who said, "*I am the vine; you are the branches. ...apart from Me you can do nothing*" (John 15:2-8).

This principle is also communicated in God's command to Adam in Genesis 2:17 when He stated: "*You must not eat from the tree of the knowledge of good and evil, for when you eat of it you will surely die.*" God really meant: "*The day you rebel or detach yourself from your Source, you will cancel your full potential. You will never fulfill the purpose for which I created you.*" Sin, therefore, can be understood as man's declaration of independence from his Source. Please note that even as trees gradually die after having their roots separated from the soil, so Adam, after disobeying his Source, died spiritually. Though Adam's spiritual death was instant, the physical effects of that death were not manifested until 930 years later. This is evidence that no matter how far man progresses or how much he accomplishes, he can never experience his full potential without a personal relationship with God, his Source.

God's concept of *death* is also defined in His words to Adam: "*...the day* that you eat of it you shall *surely die*" (Genesis 2:16 NAS). Yet when Adam did eat from the tree, he lived physically over 900 years. Every man is born detached from God—he is spiritually dead. So every man born of woman (male/female) has no awareness of his true potential, because the only sure way to know your potential is to know your Source.

The key to knowing your true potential is to know your Source. You will never understand, realize or maximize your true and full potential without a relationship with your Source. A man without a relationship with God (his Source) has limited his potential. He can never attain what he is capable of.

Exploring the Potential of Man's Triune Self— Body, Soul and Spirit

Man is a triune being created after the image and likeness of his Creator-Source. He consists of three distinct yet intricately related dimensions. Each dimension is designed to fulfill a specific purpose in God's plan for His creation. Each realm of man is designed with the potential to maximize its function and fulfill its intended purpose. But the potential of each dimension cannot be understood apart from its Source. Let us now take a closer look at each part of man and explore the untapped potential that lies buried there.

The Potential of the Body

As man, in his pursuit of knowledge about his world and environment (through the disciplines of science), explores the various aspects of creation, he reaches the general conclusion that the magnificent mystery of the human body still stands at the apex of all natural forms of creation. For decades, specialists have dedicated their lives to the study of the physiological potential of the human body—its ability to handle pressure; to adjust itself to varying environmental changes; to defend itself against disease, danger or threat; to maintain its stamina under physical exertion. Yet, despite man's technological advancements and his scientific explorations of this masterpiece of creation, scientists continue to admit that they have limited knowledge concerning the potential of this mechanism of precision we call *the human body*.

The human body has been described as eighty percent water (fluid), with a degree of calcium, fibre and tissue. But to fully appreciate the true potential of the human body, we must understand the *purpose* for its creation.

The Purpose of the Body

To understand the purpose of the body, we must understand the purpose for man. When God created man, He created him a *spirit* being with a *physical* house (body). Then God placed him on the *physical* earth. God purposed and intended to rule and dominate the physical realm from the invisible realm through the agency of *mankind*. In essence, God desired to control the *seen* from the *unseen* through the *unseen* living in the *seen* on the *seen*. God desired to have His Kingdom extended from heaven to earth by allowing His Spirit to reign through man's spirit as man dominated the earth through his soul and manifested His nature through the body. Therefore, the triune nature of man is designed for the following purposes:

1. **Man's spirit:**   **To relate to God (pick up the spirit world)**

2. **Man's soul:**   **To relate to the mental realm (intelligence)**

3. **Man's body:**   **To relate to the physical environment (pick up earth)**

The human body was thus specifically designed to relate to and pick up the earth or physical realm. God did not intend the body to relate to the spiritual or supernatural world. It is essential, then, that we do not judge our true potential by the abilities or limitations of our physical bodies. For this reason, our five senses are specifically designed to "pick up" our natural environment. Our powers of sight, touch, hearing, smell and taste are all related to the natural, physical world. The potential of our bodies is therefore governed by its physical capabilities. God never intended man to be controlled or limited by his physical body. You were not created to be intimidated by your environment.

From Revelation to Information— From Discernment to Sense

Man's original state in the garden of Eden, before the fall, was one of perfect union and fellowship with God. He was designed to live from the *inside* to the *outside*, from his *spirit* to his *body*. God designed man to be *led* by his spirit, not *driven* by his environment. Man was intended to live through spiritual *discernment*, not physical *senses*. But when Adam (the first man) disobeyed God, he destroyed his fellowship and communion with the Spirit of God (Genesis 3). The consequence was death.

Death is isolation from the spirit world of God. Through disobedience, man's spirit lost contact with the source of heaven. As a result, man became a victim of his *soul* (mind, will, emotions) and his *body* (five senses). His life became governed by his external environment as his five senses controlled his existence.

Immediately after Adam and Eve disobeyed God's command, "the eyes of both of them were opened, and they *knew* that they were naked" (Genesis 3:7 NAS). The word *knew* comes from the concept *to know*, from which we get our word *knowledge*. In essence, Adam and Eve suddenly became aware of their external environment. They began to live life from the knowledge they gained from their *senses*. That was the birth of *education*.

From that day on, man measured his life, worth and value by his environment. And the relationship between man and his environment gave birth to humanistic philosophy. In reality, the body and its sensual capacity became man's measure of reality. Man started living and interpreting his existence according to the *information* he gained through the senses of his *body*, instead of the *revelation* received through his spirit from the Spirit of God. Man's fall placed his body in a position it had not been designed to occupy. This change has caused man to limit his potential ability to the capabilities of his senses and his physical body.

Dignified Dirt

No matter how majestic and wonderful the human body is, we must be careful to remember the reality of its composition. According to Genesis 2:7, the Manufacturer of this magnificent masterpiece made and formed it from the "*dust of the ground.*" The body is one hundred percent *dirt*. The apostle Paul called the body a "[heavenly] treasure in earthen vessels" (2 Corinthians 2:7). The principle we discussed earlier—the potential of a thing is related to its source—must be considered. If the physical body is related to the earth, it must be sustained and maintained by the earth. The body must feed on soil (dirt) in order to live (plants, animals, fish, etc.). We must, therefore, understand that our bodies—though they have tremendous potentials, powers, capabilities and values—must never become the full measure of our potential.

Physical Handicap—Myth or Master

There are millions of physically handicapped individuals who, because of their society's concept of potential, have resigned themselves to a life of self-pity, depression and isolation. There are many who have confused their bodies with their true selves. They have mistaken the "house" for the "resident."

But history gives ample evidence of thousands who have freed themselves of the myth that their bodies should dictate their true potential. They have defied the limitations of their "dirt houses" and soared to the unlimited heights of their soul's and spirit's potential. Many have turned their wheelchairs into the cockpits of jetliners as they explored the heights of their capabilities. Other have used their walking canes to pole-vault them into positions that changed the world. Some transformed their world of silence to produce sounds that many are enjoying today. Still others have used their blindness to see beyond the physical. They have captured sights others long to see.

Helen Keller refused to be blinded by others' opinions of her ability—she changed the attitude of the world. Sir Winston Churchill refused to be muted by his speech impediment and physical handicap—while a member of the British Parliament and later the Prime Minister of Britain, he delivered some of history's most life-changing orations.

What is your handicap? Is it a wheelchair, a bed, a walker, the socio-economic status of your family or the color of your skin? Is it the ghetto, your parents' lifestyle, the level of your education or a terminal illness? Are you disabled by divorce, the absence of your parents, incest or child abuse? Are you blind or deaf? Do you have a speech impediment or a poor self-esteem? Whatever your *perceived* handicap may be, you must never allow your true potential to become a victim of the limitations of your physical body or your environment. Reach beyond your grasp. Your body is not your full potential.

Reach beyond your grasp.
Your body is not your full potential.

I encourage you to develop and maintain a correct attitude toward your body. Learn to see it from the perspective of God, its Creator, who (through the apostle Paul) calls it "the temple of the living God" (2 Corinthians 6:16). God admonishes you to keep your temple holy, clean and healthy. You are the steward of this precious earthly vessel. Its maintenance and effective operation are your responsibility. Like any essential equipment, your body needs regular checkups, proper amounts of fuel (food), periods of recuperation and recreation (rest, sleep and fasting), and invigorating exercise. But do not allow your body to become the dictator of your potential. You are not your body.

The biblical perspective on the body is revealed in a number of clear declarations:

Do you not know that your body is a temple of the Holy Spirit, who is in you...? ... Therefore honor God with your body (1 Corinthians 6:19).

Therefore we do not lose heart. Though outwardly we are wasting away, yet inwardly we are being renewed day by day (2 Corinthians 4:16).

Please note that the previous reference describes the physical body as being in a state of daily disintegration. If we determine our potential by the condition of our bodies—whether we are handicapped or relatively healthy and fit—we are still relying on a premise that is constantly dissolving. You and I must not allow any physical impediment or the natural aging process to immobilize the potential that lies within us.

One of the greatest figures in history is described in the Bible as "the father of the faithful." Abraham demonstrated the tremendous potential of the soul and the spirit, in contrast to the limited potential of the body. The apostle Paul writes,

As it is written: "I have made you a father of many nations." He is our father in the sight of God, in whom he
believed... Against all hope, Abraham in hope believed
and so became the father of many nations.... Without
wavering in his faith, he faced the fact that his body was
as good as dead...being fully persuaded that God had the
power to do what He had promised (Romans 6:17-21).

The key to Abraham's success is related to his attitude
toward his body. The demands made upon him by God were
beyond the natural capacity of his physical body. He was
handicapped by age and his wife was handicapped by a bar-
ren womb. But they considered not their bodies and
believed that God had provided the potential to fulfill the
demand being placed upon them. You must refuse to limit
your true potential by the limitations of your physical body.

The Potential of the Soul

Some years ago a famous pop singer sang a song entitled
"I'm a Soul Man." That title became a common phrase
throughout the western world. I suspect he was referring to
the cultural-ethnic orientation of the Afro-American artistic
expression. But the statement communicates both a statement of truth and a myth. As we discussed earlier in this
chapter, the *soul* is the triunity of the *mind*, the *will* and the
emotions. The soul was created for the purpose of receiving
revelation from the spirit-man to communicate it to the body
and *information* from the physical senses to transmit it to
the spirit-man. In essence, the soul was designed to be the
"*servant*" of the spirit-man, and the body was designed to be
the "*servant*" of the soul. Man is a spirit, lives in a body and
possesses a soul. But the fall of man changed that.

**Man is a spirit, lives in a body
and possesses a soul.**

When Adam disobeyed God's words, his spirit lost fellowship with God's Spirit and was paralyzed. The soul became a victim of his body and the physical senses. When *revelation* from the spirit-man was replaced by *information* from the physical senses, man became a victim of his environment with education as his primary goal. In fact, man was reduced to a "soul man." Never allow a teacher's opinion or the score on an academic test or the fact that you didn't complete your formal education to dictate the magnitude of your potential. You are as potent as your Creator says you are. The exercise of the soul can make you smart, but not wise. Paul states in 1 Corinthians 1:25: "The foolishness of God is wiser than man's wisdom and the weakness of God is stronger than man's strength."

The Potential of Your Spirit

The measure of your true potential is your *spirit*. God has always intended that you and I would live from the inside—from the spirit-man in communion with the eternal *Spirit of God*. Without that relationship, you are limited to the potential of your soul and your body. The apostle Paul in his letter to the church at Rome wrote:

> The *mind* of sinful man is death, but the *mind* controlled by the Spirit is life and peace (Romans 8:6).

Please note that the Bible says that *the mind controlled by the spirit* is like a fountain of life gushing forth with the potential of God through the Spirit of God. Paul also writes:

> Those who live according to the sinful nature have their minds set on what that nature desires; but those who live in accordance with the *Spirit* have their minds set on what the *Spirit* desires (Romans 8:5).

The Spirit of God has some desires. I believe these desires are God's original predestined will for your life as written in the book described in Psalm 139:16. If you allow the Holy Spirit to fellowship with and minister to your spirit, and you remain hooked up to the Source of your potential, then you will live according to the knowledge of God's revelation of your true potential. There are things in God's mind concerning you that your soul can never receive, because it cannot discern them. God has information on your ability and potential that will astonish you and your family. Paul mentions this in 1 Corinthians 2:9-11:

> However it is written: "No eye has seen, no ear has heard, no mind has conceived what God has prepared for those who love him"—but God has revealed it to us by *His Spirit*. The Spirit searches all things, even the deep things of God. For who among men knows the thoughts of a man except the man's spirit within him? In the same way no one knows the *thoughts* of God except the *Spirit* of God.

Whether you are young or old, rich or poor, black or white, a college graduate or a high-school dropout, you are still a treasure of potential. The measure of your true potential is hidden in the Spirit of God. It can only be tapped by a relationship between your spirit and His. Go after the deep things in God that are related to you as the deep of your potential calls to the deep of the *Omni-potent* One. Decide to discover God's concept of your potential.

PRINCIPLES

---

1. The key to knowing your true potential is to know your Source—God.

2. Man is a triune being: body, soul and spirit.

3. The spirit is intended to relate to God, the soul to the mental realm and the body to the physical environment.

4. Death is isolation from the spirit world. We are spiritually dead at our physical birth.

5. Your body is not the measure of your true potential.

6. Your soul (mind, will and emotions) is not the measure of your true potential.

7. The measure of your true potential is your spirit.

8. God's desires for your life are discerned by your spirit through fellowship and communication with the Holy Spirit.

11 | Keys to Fulfilling Your True Potential

What lies behind us and what lies before us are tiny matters, compared to what lies *within* us.

Oliver Wendel Holmes

Now to Him who is able to do immeasurably more than all we ask or imagine, according to His power that is at work within us...

Apostle Paul, Ephesians 3:20

Do you read manuals? Any manufacturer of a piece of equipment—a refrigerator, a microwave, a television, a toaster, a sewing machine, a washing machine—gives you a manual when you buy their product. When you open the manual, the first thing you read is: Before plugging in this product, read this manual carefully. But most of us don't, right? I know I don't. Then if you turn to the first page of the manual you find a description of the product and often a picture as well describing the various parts and what they can do. The next page usually tells you what you can expect from the product. Finally they tell you: If something goes wrong with this product, do not fix it yourself. Take it to a qualified technician who has the certification from this manufacturer to fix it. If you don't, the warranty on this product is null and void.

If you want a piece of equipment to operate at its maximum potential, you have to follow the manufacturer's instructions. If you don't follow the instructions, you may damage the product—or at least you won't know what you can expect from it. Only if you follow the instructions can you expect the product to meet the demands specified by the manufacturer—demands that equal what the manufacturer designed and built into the product.

God's Instruction Manual

We are excellent, complexly designed, tremendously built, intricately put together pieces of equipment. But we don't know what we can do. We can't even imagine the full extent of our potential. Knowing this, God sent us a manual that contains a description of our parts. He said, "Now this first part is your spirit and the second part is your soul and the third part is your body. Now here is what the body is supposed to do...here is what the soul can do...here is what the spirit can do." God also tells us the potential of this equipment called human beings. In His manual, He lists all the things we are capable of doing.

When God first presented this piece of equipment called man, something went wrong. Instead of taking it back to the manufacturer to be fixed, we took it to a second-rate, second-class, unskilled technician. And look what he did. He muddled the job. We submitted God's equipment and product to satan, who is an unauthorized dealer with no genuine parts.

But God loved us so much that, even though the warranty had run out, He decided to take back the product. Though someone else has tried to fix us and has messed us up, God is starting all over again—and He's putting in His own parts. God is rebuilding and remaking us. He knows us better than anybody else, because He is our Creator. His Word, the Bible, reveals much about His attitude toward our potential.

God's Word on Your Potential

You have the potential to be in God's class.

> **So God created man in His own image; in the image of God He created him; male and female He created them** (Genesis 1:27).

God sees you as being in His class. Because He made you in His image, you have the potential to be in the God class—which is spirit.

You have the potential to operate like God.

> **Then God said, "Let Us make man in Our image, in Our likeness..."** (Genesis 1:26)

When God made you in His likeness, He did not make you to *look* like Him. He made you to *function* like Him. That's what *likeness* literally means. When God created you, He made you to operate like Him. If you are not functioning like God, you are "malfunctioning," because God wired and designed you to function like Him. How does God function? His Word says, "Without faith it is impossible to please God" (Hebrews 11:6). God functions by faith. You and I were designed to operate by faith. Our potential therefore needs faith in order to be maximized.

God sees in you the potential to dominate, rule and subdue the whole earth.

> [God said] **"...let them rule over the fish of the sea and the birds of the air, over the livestock, over all the earth,**

and over all the creatures that move along the ground."
... God blessed them and said to them "...Rule over the
fish of the sea and the birds of the air and over every
living creature that moves on the ground" (Genesis
1:26,28).

God created you to rule over all the earth and everything
that creeps in it. He will never demand anything of you He
didn't already build into you. Thus, if the earth in any way
is dominating you, you are malfunctioning. You were not
created to give into cigarettes or submit to alcohol. God did
not intend for you to be controlled by drugs, sex, money,
power or greed. If any of these are governing you, you are
living below your privilege. Because God has already
declared it to be so, you have the ability to dominate the
earth. Everything in the earth must be under your subjec-
tion, not mastering you.

**You have the ability to be fruitful and reproduce after
your kind.**

God blessed them and said to them, "Be fruitful and
increase in number; fill the earth and subdue it" (Genesis
1:28).

Again God is calling forth something that's already in
you. He didn't tell the man and the woman to *try* to be
fruitful, He simply told them to *do* it. He knew they already
had the ability to multiply and reproduce and fill the earth.
You too can reproduce yourself. He always places the potential inside before He calls it forth. Whatever God calls you
to do, He has already built in.

You have the ability to imagine and plan to do anything.

The Lord said, "If as one people speaking the same language they have begun to do this, then nothing they plan
to do will be impossible for them" (Genesis 11:6).

God gave you the ability to imagine and plan and bring into being anything you desire. Now if you read this passage in its entirety, the people to whom God was talking had planned to build a tower. God didn't stop them from building a tower by cutting off their potential. He stopped them by confusing their language, because He couldn't stop their potential. You have the same potential God saw in those people. If you decide to do something, and you believe in it hard enough and commit yourself to work for it long enough, nothing in the universe can stop you. That's what God is saying. If you want to do anything, God already said, "You can do it." Only if you lack the commitment to follow after your dream will your dream remain unfinished. The potential to do and plan anything is in you if you will believe and persevere.

You have the potential to believe impossibilities into possibilities.

Everything is possible for him who believes (Mark 9:23).

Not only are you able to plan, but you also have the ability to believe something that seems impossible and actually make it possible. If you can abandon yourself to an idea and sacrifice all you have for that idea, God says, "It's possible for that idea to come to pass."

You have the potential to influence physical and spiritual matter.

I will give to you the keys of the kingdom of heaven; whatever you bind on earth will be bound in heaven, and whatever you loose on earth will be loosed in heaven (Matthew 16:19).

Jesus is talking here about your power to influence what's on earth as well as what's in heaven. If you bind something on earth, it will be bound in heaven. You have influence in heaven. Likewise, if you loose something on earth, heaven has to do the same thing—loose it. You have the power to influence things in both realms of earth and heaven. You may never have imagined that you possess that kind of power. But Jesus says you do.

You have the potential to receive whatever you ask.

> If you remain in Me and My words remain in you, ask whatever you wish, and it will be given you (John 15:7).

God says you have the potential to receive whatever you ask. That's frightening. You have a blank check—but there is one condition on the cashing of that check: You must abide in Christ, and His words must abide in you. If that condition is met, you can ask anything in Jesus' name and it will be done for you. Jesus wants to knock the limits off your mind. But first He requires that you stay hooked up with God. Then He says, "Go ahead and ask me for anything. I'll do whatever you ask." What potential! That's God's word on *you*.

You have the potential to do greater works than Jesus did.

> I tell you the truth, anyone who has faith in Me will do what I have been doing. He will do even greater things than these, because I am going to the Father (John 14:12).

Jesus sees in you the potential to do greater things than He did. And He means what He says. For many years I didn't want to read that scripture because I knew that what Jesus said and what was really happening were two different things. But if Jesus says you have that potential, it's in there somewhere. Remember, whatever God says, you can do. He won't ask you to do anything He hasn't already wired you to do.

God believes in you. He knows the vastness of your potential. If He gives you an assignment, He's already given you the ability to fulfill what He asks. Along with His *demand* always comes the *capability* to meet that demand. But remember: To release your potential, you must be related to your Source. Only as you are connected to God, can you fulfill and maximize your true potential.

Say "Yes" To Jesus

Sin, or rebellion against God, clogs up our potential. Disobedience to God may have stunted your capacity for growth. But God sees and cares about that problem. He sent Jesus into the world to die for you. Jesus doesn't have a problem knowing who He is and what He can do. *You* have that problem. Jesus came to die so *you* can know who you are and what is the fullness of *your* potential. He came to open up the capacity of who you are—to unclog your true self.

Calvary is God's way of providing the means to unplug your true potential. Because disobedience has capped off your potential, God offers you forgiveness and hope through Jesus Christ. In your plugged up state, you can't begin to touch your true ability. Only after you say "yes" to Jesus (and your spirit begins to communicate and fellowship again with the Holy Spirit) can you start the journey of fulfilling all the potential God planted within you before you were born.

It is my earnest desire that you will realize the awesome wealth of potential residing in you. But more important than this potential is the necessity that you understand your need for a personal relationship with Your Creator through the agency He has provided, Jesus Christ. I encourage you to pray the following prayer with me in faith:

Dear heavenly Father, Creator and Manufacturer of my life, today I submit my life to You, totally surrendering the product of my whole life to You for complete repair, maintenance and renewal in Jesus Christ. I confess Him as the only Savior of my life and submit to Him as my Lord. By faith I this moment receive the Holy Spirit, who, by His power, makes me an eternal citizen of Your Kingdom of Heaven. I commit myself to serve and acknowledge You in all my ways as I endeavor to maximize my potential for Your praise and glory...

This I pray in Jesus' Name
Amen.

After praying this prayer, please write to me and allow me to share your joy. I will write to you and send you some helpful material. (My address is on the last page of this book.)

Ten Keys to Releasing Your Potential

At this point, you must be aware of the tremendous wealth of potential locked away inside of you crying out for exposure and fulfillment. I believe you have heard the voices of your childhood dreams and the many visions, goals and plans you once had screaming out for resurrection. Now the big question remains: How do I release this potential?

Every manufacturer establishes the specifications, environment, conditions and operational standards for attaining the maximum performance level of his product. God our Creator and Manufacturer has also establised a plan—environment, conditions, standards and specifications—for the maximum performance and release of your potential. After many years of careful study and practice, I have identified ten major keys to releasing your full potential.

Violation of any one of these requirements will result in the malfuntion, distortion, misuse and abuse of your precious potential. The keys to releasing your potential follow:

Key #1—You must know (be related to) your Source.

It is essential that you understand the nature, composition and consistency of your Source, because this is the key to understanding the potency of your potential. If you, for example, had a wooden table in your house, you would be aware that the table is made of wood from a tree. The strength, durability and nature of the table can only be as strong and durable as the tree. If the tree is weak, the table will be the same. Therefore, the potential of the table is determined by the potential of the source from which it came.

The same is true for you. To understand how much potential you possess, you must understand the Source from which you came. You and I possess all the qualities and nature of our Source and are capable of manifesting these qualities. We also possess an eternal spirit just like our Source. We will live forever—not because He allows us to, but because it's our nature.

But where you spend your forever is determined by you. A manufacturer's product must remain related to its source in order to be maintained and supplied with genuine parts and authorized service. It is this relationship that manufacturing companies call the *warranty/guarantee* agreement, in which the product has to be subjected to the conditions, specifications and operational standards set by the manufacturer if he is to take responsibility for the maximum performance, maintenance and servicing of the product. Violation of the manufacturer's conditions and standards cancels the warranty/guarantee relationship and places the product at the mercy of unauthorized dealers.

The same relationship exists between *God* and *man*. God guarantees the maximum performance of our potential if we remain related to Him and submit to the conditions, specifications and standards set by Him. A personal relationship with our Creator is a necessary key to the releasing of our full potential.

Key #2—You must understand how the product was designed to function.

Every manufacturer designs, develops and produces his product to function in a specific manner. Automobile manufacturers design their products to function with gasoline, sparkplugs, batteries, pistons, oil, water, etc. No matter what you do, if you do not supply the elements required for the operational function of the product, it will not perform and maximize its potential.

God created man and designed him to function like He does. You and I were created to function *by faith and love*. Without faith, it is impossible to please God. These are the fuels on which we run. That which is not of faith is sin for us. The just live (operate) by *faith*. Our potential cannot be released without faith and love. Fear and hatred cause the short-circuit of our potential.

Key #3—You must know your purpose.

Every product exists for a specific purpose. That reason is the original intent of its existence—the purpose for which the manufacturer made it. This is an essential key because the purpose for which something was made determines its design, nature and potential.

God created you and gave you birth for a purpose. Whatever that purpose is, you possess the potential to fulfill it. No matter how big the dream God gave you, your potential is equal to the assignment. Purpose gives birth to responsibility, and responsibility makes demands on potential.

Key #4—You must understand your resources.

All manufacturers provide access to the necessary resources for the proper maintenance, sustenance and operation of their products. Resources and provisions are to help sustain the product while its potential is being maximized.

God, in His great wisdom, provided for human beings tremendous material and physical resources to sustain and maintain us as we proceed in realizing, developing and maximizing our potential. *Resources* were created to live *on* and *with*, but never *for*. We are never to worship the resources, nor are we to become controlled by them. Idolatry and substance and drug abuse are violations of the Manufacturer's specifications, and will lead to the destruction of potential.

Key #5—You must have the right environment.

Environment consists of the conditions that have a direct or indirect effect on the performance, function and development of a thing. These conditions can be internal and external. Every manufacturer specifies the proper conditions under which he guarantees the maximum performance of the potential of the product. In the manual, the manufacturer will caution against violation of that specified environment for maximum performance. The right environment is the ideal conditions needed for the maximization of the true potential.

God created everything to flourish within a specific environment. Plants, animals and fish all need a specific environment in order to live. Potential is nullified, aborted and destroyed when the environment is violated or disrupted. This is also true of man.

God designed man to function in the garden (His presence), in relationship with Him, free from sin and in daily communion with His Spirit. Man's potential needs this positive environment of fellowship, relationship, love and challenge in order to be maximized. You can never be all you could be in any other environment. The fall of man contaminated his environment and poisoned the atmosphere of our potential. It produced abnormal behavior and the malfuntion of the human factor. The key to releasing your true potential is the restoration of God's original environment. Jesus came to restore us to the Father. He sent the Holy Spirit to restore our internal environment.

Key #6—You must work out your potential.

Potential is dormant ability. But ability is useless until it is given reponsibility. When God created man, He planted in him the potential to multiply and fill the earth and subdue, dominate and rule the earth and everything in it. Man's potential was predetermined by this purpose. He had inside him all the potential necessary to fulfill the assignment. But he was not aware of his potential, even as you may not be aware of what you can do. Therefore, the first thing God gave the man was not a wife, but *work* (Genesis 2:15). He made demands on the potential of man's mind by commanding him to name the animals, and stimulated the potential of his body by commanding him to cultivate the garden. God gave man insight into the potential of his spirit by commanding him to dominate the whole earth for God.

Work is a major key to releasing your potential. Potential must be exercised and demands made on it, otherwise it will remain potential. Claiming a promise does not make it happen. You must apply the principle of work. The land was promised to Abraham, but he had to walk it out to possess it. Good ideas do not bring success. Good hard work does. To release your true potential, you must be willing to work.

Key #7—You must cultivate your potential.

Potential is like a seed. It is buried ability and hidden power that need to be cultivated. You must feed your potential the fertilizer of good positive company, give it the environment of encouragement, pour out the water of the Word of God, and bathe it in the sunshine of personal prayer. Read materials that stimulate your faith and nourish your dream.

Key #8—You must guard your potential.

It is tragic when a tree dies in a seed or a man dies in a boy. It is sad when what could have been becomes what should have been. With all the wealth of your potential, you must be careful to guard and protect it. The command to protect was among the first commands God gave to Adam. The Bible calls your potential a *treasure* in earthen vessels. You must guard your visions and dreams from sin, discouragement, procrastination, failures, opinions, distractions, traditions and compromise. Satan is after your potential. Be on guard.

Key #9—You must share your potential.

God created the entire heavens and earth with the potential principle, which can only be fulfilled when it is shared. Nature abounds with this truth. The sun does not exist for itself. Plants release oxyen for us and we give carbon dioxide to the plants. The bee receives necture as it pollinates the flowers. No potential exists for itself. This is also true of man. True potential and fulfillment in life is not what is accomplished, but who benefits from them. Your deposit was given to enrich and inspire the lives of others. Remember, the great law is *love*.

Key #10—You must know and understand the laws of limitation.

Freedom and power are two of the most important elements in our lives. Potential is the essence of both. Potential is power. But freedom needs law to be enjoyed, and power needs responsibility to be effective. One without the other produces self-destruction. Every manufacturer establishes laws of limitations for his products. These laws are not given to restrict but to protect—not to hinder but to assist and guarantee the full and maximum performance of potential.

God has set laws and standards to protect our potential and to secure our success. Obedience is protection for potential.

All the above keys and principles are proven throughout human history to be true. Any violation of these laws limits the release and maximization of your potential. Commit yourself to obeying the Manufacturer. Then watch your life unfold as you discover the hidden ability that was always within you.

12 | Dare to Believe in Your Potential

Human potential without godly purpose produces self-destruction.

The Bible tells us a story about people who decided to build a city with a tower that reached to the heavens. They wanted to *"make a name"* for themselves. When God saw how committed the builders were to their task He said, "...nothing they plan to do will be impossible for them." So He came down and confused their languages so they couldn't work together. That stopped their building (Genesis 11:8).

Do you think God was against the tower? No. God was against the goal of the tower. They did not have a relationship with God. They were ungodly men and women who intended to build a tower to heaven so *their* name could be great. They weren't interested in making God's name great, they wanted to make a name for themselves.

When God saw how committed they were to their task, He knew He had to stop them. Otherwise, they would be able to do anything they wanted to. God made this declaration to men who had no relationship with Him. Yet He saw in them the potential to do much. He knew the potential, ability and untapped power He had placed within all men.

Think then what you can do if you are hooked up with your Source. Jesus came into the world to reestablish your connection with God. He came to show you who you really are underneath the cap of sin and disobedience. He came to teach you how to look beyond the realm of the visible into the unseen sphere of faith.

What Are You Doing With Your Potential?

Man has accomplished many things without God. Many inventors in the world are ungodly people. Most of the people who do great feats and accomplish great exploits are ungodly people. Imagine what would happen if they were hooked up with God. Jesus came to provide that hookup. When God saw what we could and should do, it disappointed Him that we were not aware of it. So He paid the greatest price necessary—the cost of His own life—to release our full potential. Then He said, "Now go on, son. Do all you can dream. If you can think it, daughter, you can do it."

**God paid the greatest price necessary—
the cost of His own life—
to release our full potential.**

Yet many of us still live below the level of our true ability. We have settled for the standards established by the opinions of others regarding our potential. We are afraid to move beyond our dreams to action. It is more comfortable to think about all we *might* do instead of working to achieve what we *can* do. People who change the world are people who stop dreaming and wake up. They don't just wish, they act.

If you have accepted Jesus as your Lord and Savior, I'm here to encourage you to move on with the real things of God. What have you done since you were saved? What have you accomplished?

Life Is More Than Shelter, Food or Security

Maslow, one of the greatest influences on the thought patterns of psychology in our world, theorized that man is driven by his base needs. He believed that your most immediate need becomes your controlling factor. Therefore, your first instinct is to find shelter, secondly food and thirdly security or protection. Then you begin to move up the ladder of becoming self-realized and self-actualized, of getting self-esteem and all the rest of that stuff. According to this theory, human beings are driven by their base needs.

In the sixth chapter of Matthew, Jesus challenges that thought pattern. He instructs us to live from the perspective of what exists that we cannot see, instead of being totally caught up in the details and needs of our daily lives. God lives and thinks in the potential. He always see things that have not yet been manifested. Faith too lives in the potential—not in the present. Jesus simply asks us to have faith—to believe in God's goodness and care.

In the Matthew setting, Jesus was talking to His disciples, not to the multitudes. His words were for people who had already left home and car and family and everything to follow Him. But He says, "Here you are. You've left children. You've given up your job. You say you love Me, but yet you worry. Don't you know that God is aware of all your needs? Don't you see how He takes care of the birds of the air and the grass of the field? How much more precious you are to your heavenly Father than these. Stop worrying. Stop babbling on like the pagans. You are supposed to be living in

God's Kingdom. I have come into the world to reestablish and build back God's Kingdom."

Stop worrying.

In teaching His followers that food, drink, clothes and shelter are not the most important things in life, Jesus directly contradicts the psychological theories of our world. He dares you to follow God and think in the opposite. God doesn't start with your wants, but with who you are. God wants you to first know who you are. Then you will realize you deserve the things. In God's design, you deserve the things because you are somebody.

According to God, Maslow was wrong—and I go with God. There are people who have everything, but they still don't know who they are. People accumulate things with the hope that the things will make them somebody. But you don't become somebody by accumulating things. Ask the guy at the top who can't sleep. Ask the guy who has everything except peace and love and joy in his heart. Maslow was wrong. God desires to give you self-worth and self-esteem first. He wants you to know who you are first.

You Don't Need Things to Enjoy Life— You Need Life to Enjoy Things

I have met so many people who have everything except the knowledge of who they are. Jesus said, "Why worry about these things? Life is so much more than these things about which you worry. Life is peace and love and joy and patience and gentleness..."

Seek first the things of God and everything else you need will just fall into place. The mind controlled by the Spirit of God is full of life and peace. Peace is so important to a fulfilled life. It goes hand in hand with the life Jesus came to bring. You don't have to worry when you know what is coming. When you live by the Spirit in the realm of the unseen and the invisible, there is no reason to worry. God is holding what is in store for you, because all things that are, were and are in God.

**Seek first the things of God
and everything else you need
will just fall into place.**

If you'll let Him, God will work it all out for you. Through your spirit talking with His Spirit, He'll assure you everything is going to be okay. You don't have to worry if God's already told you how a particular situation is going to turn out. Relax and commit yourself to maximize your potential. Preoccupy yourself with this assignment and purpose for your life, knowing that whatever God asks for He provides for.

What's Really Important?

When we are distracted by our drive for personal security and our search for identity, we rarely achieve our true potential. Our search for things, what we can relate to through our senses and our minds, harasses us and keeps us so busy trying to make a living that we don't have time to live. We are so caught up trying to make it *through* life that we don't have time to be *in* life.

Have you ever seen people who work all day, every day and then suddenly they realize they've grown old and can no longer enjoy life? They have missed living because they were so busy trying to make one. Jesus tells you to seek first a relationship with the Spirit of God; these things that are distracting you will then become a normal part of His provisions for your life.

The Kingdom of God comes when you are hooked up again to God. Then God can flow through you all He has desired for you since before you were born. The Kingdom of God is coming back under God's leadership—His government—so your true potential is unbound and released. God wants all He stored in you to blossom and flourish. He longs for the relationship between your spirit and His Holy Spirit to prosper so you can reveal the limitless depths of the wealth of your hidden potential. God never put anything into you that was not supposed to come out of you. His joy is fulfilled when you show off His glory—the real nature of who God is.

You came out of God. He created you to look and think and act like Him so you would display His greatness, majesty and sovereignty. The summit of God's desires for your life is that you will show through your being who He is.

Your potential is not determined by what you look like or how far you went in school. Nor is it determined by what others think and expect from you? God, your Creator, determines the extent of your ability. Through the Holy Spirit, He enables you to develop and experience your entire potential. God makes it possible for you to do and be much more than anyone (including you) expects. You may not look smart, but if the One who made you demands smartness from you, it's in there somewhere.

Potential Produces Faith—
Faith Is Knowing Potential Is There

In the beginning, everything that is, was in God. Before anything was, it already existed in God. Everything we see existed in the invisible state before God made it visible. So faith is not geared to what does not exist—it relates to everything that is not seen. Faith is "being sure of what we hope for and certain of what we do not see" (Hebrews 11:1). It deals with potential—what you yet can see, do, be and experience. Faith says, "I can't see it, but I believe it is there." Faith never deals with what you have done, but with what you yet could do.

God is stuffed with many things and He's waiting for you to ask Him for everything you need. But you have to ask with faith, because faith is the stuff that deals with unseen things. Faith is not some spooky experience. It's simply knowing that what you can't see is there.

Can you imagine waking up every day, with all your problems, knowing that whatever you see is not the real story? Can you even imagine living that way—looking not at things that can be seen, but at the things that are not seen? What we see is temporary. It's those things we can't see that are eternal. Living by faith requires looking at the unseen, because everything that is, was in God; and *everything you could be is in you now, waiting for you to make demands on it by faith in God.*

Wishing Is Not Enough—Dare to Desire

Therefore I say unto you, What things soever ye desire, when ye pray, believe that ye receive them, and ye shall have them (Mark 11:24 KJV).

Very often the Church has misread this word *desire*. We have expected, perhaps, that the word *desire* means "what we are dreaming about." No. *Desire* is "craving enough to sacrifice for." Only if we are willing to die for what we desire will we receive it.

Desire is "craving enough to sacrifice for."

How often have you had a good idea and done nothing about it because you didn't desire it bad enough? When we want something so bad we can taste it, an urgency energizes our efforts. This is extremely important for your faith, because faith is what you are asking for but can't yet see. A strong desire enables you to stand your ground until you see what you have believed. There are only a few who are gutsy enough to live in this manner. How much do you really desire the goals you have set for your life?

God is pregnant with everything that isn't yet visible—including what you ask for in prayer. When you ask for something in faith, it is already on the way. You can't see it, but if you believe, it is already in process. God wants you to ask many things of Him, because He is stuffed with many blessings and abilities that He wants to come out.

Thus, whatever you *desire* when you pray, you shall have—*but only what you desire*. Not what you *pray* for—only what you *desire when you pray*. There are many things we ask God for in prayer that we don't really desire. We don't crave them at the expense of life. We don't want them bad enough to sacrifice for them. We just hope God does it. If it happens, praise the Lord—if it doesn't happen, praise the Lord. When you pray with this attitude, you don't really want what you prayed for. If you truly want something when you pray, Jesus says you'll get up and knock and seek and run out until you get it (Matthew 7:7-8). If you are serious about *desiring* what you pray for, you will get up off your knees and go do it.

Your Desire Controls Your Direction in Life

Many people get distracted in life because they do not desire anything enough to keep on course. If you do not set a goal for your potential and say, "Look, I don't care what anybody says. That's what I want to become," you might as well forget it. You must have a goal that you desire so strongly you will go after it no matter what the expense. If you are not willing to do that, you have lost already, because it is your desire for the thing that will keep you on the road of consistency. Potential needs desire to place demands upon it.

**You must have a goal you desire
so strongly you will go after it
no matter what the expense.**

This life is full of advertisements for your attention. Life is crowded and jammed with distractions. They come from all sides, trying to shake you from your goal. If you don't have a goal, they will provide one for you. You must know where you want to go and what you want to become. Potential needs purpose to give it direction.

When you pray, desire what you ask for. Refuse to be distracted or interrupted. The power of your potential will be revealed as you sacrifice everything to attain what you desired in prayer.

Potential Only for the Few

Unfortunately, most of us will never fulfill the deepest desires of God's heart. Though He has done His best to free us from the false attitudes and perceptions that keep us from achieving our real potential, God is often disappointed by the lives of His creatures.

Perhaps you are a parent who has tried and tried and tried and still your kids haven't worked out. You've tried your best and given your best, but they still have disappointed you. Sometimes pastors also feel that way. They give and give and give, and the people still disappoint them. And often some of the ones who are messing up the most are the ones to whom they have given the most. Each of us feels the hurt when the people we love and have tried to help, struggle in the gutter, their lives in ruins.

In the seventh chapter of Matthew, Jesus predicts that many will hear His message, but few will follow Him and obey. Many will reject—or simply fail to accept—the abundant life He came to offer.

> Enter through the narrow gate. For wide is the gate and broad is the road that leads to destruction, and many enter through it. But small is the gate and narrow the road that leads to life, and *only a few find it* (Matthew 7:13-14).

Those words have saved my sanity. I want all who read this book to fulfill their potential; but I know only a few will. Only a minute percentage of those who hear the message about who they are will ever become all they could be. Many people will never fulfill their purpose in life. They will not be who they were supposed to be or achieve what they were designed to do. It's terrible to say, but that's why I'm sharing this with you. If only I could take my desire and put it into you, I'd do it. But I can't. Some of you will end up in the gutter because you won't receive and practice what God is telling you. I'm sorry, but it will happen. Whether you fail or succeed, win or lose, does not depend on God, but on you. He is ready to do His part if you are willing to cooperate with His purpose for your life.

Be One of the Few

Your Creator and Manufacturer built a store of miracles in you. He said you have treasures in your earthen vessel. He came to bring you abundant life. He knows there is explosive power in you waiting to be released. Through the strength of Jesus Christ you can do anything you think or imagine—and even more. But not everyone will hook up with God. Not everyone will look for the things God planted within them to be used for His glory. Not everyone will choose to fulfill their potential. Indeed, the number will be few.

I wonder which category you are in. I wonder where you are. Are you in the broad gate where everybody is going nowhere? Are you one of the many who aren't going to be anything? Come, join the narrow gate. Be one of the few. Decide you're not going with the crowd. Separate yourself, square your shoulders and do something. Choose to be somebody, instead of nobody. Leave your footprints in the sands of history and carry none of your potential to the cemetery.

Jesus passed judgment when He said, "The message my Father gave Me is for the world, but only a *few* will dare to take the challenge to handle abundant life." That's terrible. I wish that none should perish, but it is only a wish.

Are you just going to join the other guys? Are you going to be any different from the other young girls? Are you going to give into your base nature and mess up your life getting lost so no one can ever find you? Are we going to be compelled to remember you because you made your mark on history?

Can you decide that you are going to build so many monuments in people's lives that they won't have to put a stone on your grave to remind us you lived? Or are you going to be one of those people whose grave has to be marked to make sure everyone knows you used to live on this planet? Don't join the crowd—you'll get lost. Be different. Stick out like a sore thumb. Join the few.

The United States Marines established a recruiting standard that may express this attitude of the few. They say, "We just want a few good men. We don't want everybody or anybody. We want the few, the proud, the Marines." Crowds don't excite me. It's those few who I still see working on it twenty years later that excite me. They are still there plugging away. It's the few who don't allow disappointment to disarm them. They are motivated by their failure and refuse to quit until they're finished.

Are you a can-do person? Are you brave enough to face the challenge and take the risk to be effective? Will you dare to believe the impossible no matter what others say? I hope so. The world desperately needs some people who will go for the miracles no matter what it takes. The world needs some people who will believe God for the potential buried within them—desiring their dreams enough to move out and act. Only a few will find the kind of potential that allows them to live from the depths of their hidden ability. But for those who do, deep wells of possibilities will come to light as God reveals to them more and more of what He planned before the foundations of the world.

Join the few. Release the miracles hidden in your thoughts. Dare to try even after you've failed. Become reconnected to God and find out who you are and what you can do. Give your potential a chance, because God is waiting to do much more than you can think or imagine. He loves you. He wants you to be the beautiful person He created you to be.

The World Within the Third World

A Definition of the Term "Third World"

Today there are over five billion people on planet earth. Over half of these people live in countries and conditions that have been labeled *Third World*. This term was invented by a French economist who was attempting to describe the various groupings of peoples throughout the world based on their socio-economic status. Whether or not this term is valid, it is generally accepted as a description or element of identification for millions of people.

I was born and live in a part of the world that is said to fall within this category. The term is defined as any people who did not benefit from or participate in the industrial revolution. A large majority of these peole were not allowed to benefit or participate from the industrial revolution because they were subjugated at that time, being used to fuel the economic base for that revolution. Many of them were reduced to slaves and indentured servants, thus robbing them of their identity, dignity, self-worth and self-respect.

A Word to the Victims of History

Today, despite changes in conditions and a greater measure of freedom and independence, many are still grappling with their identity and their sense of self-worth. Many of the nations that progressed and developed through the industial revolution have reinforced (by attitudes, policies and legislations) the notion that these Third World peoples do not possess the potential to develop the skills, intelligence and sophistication necessary to equal that of industrialized states.

With this prejudice in mind, I wish to say to all Third World peoples everywhere—black, yellow, brown, red and white; African, American, Indian, Spanish, Latin, Arabian, Oriental and other nationalities—your potential is limitless. You possess the ability to achieve, develop, accomplish, produce, create and perform anything your mind can conceive. God created you the way you are, with all the potential you need deposited within you so you can fulfill your potential in this life. The opinions of others should never determine your self-worth. Your identity is not found in the prejudgments of others, but in the Source from which you came: God, Your Father and Creator. Jesus came to restore you to your rightful position and to reveal to you the awesome potential that is trapped inside you.

The wealth within the Third World must be realized, harnessed and maximized by its people. We must be willing to work and commit ourselves to tapping the potential within the land, our youth, the arts, sports and music. Our governments must believe that they have the ability to improve on systems and forms institutionalized by the industrialized states. The Church in the Third World must begin to take responsibility for its own people and appreciate that they have the potential to write their own songs and books and to develop an indigenous curriculum for Christian education, leadership training, resource management, and financial autonomy and accountability.

It is crucial that we do not inhibit our potential to chart a new course for the future by being destroyed by our preoccupation with the past. We have the responsibility to deposit the wealth of our potential in this generation so the next generation can build their future on our faithfulness to becoming everything we can possibly be. Just as there is a forest in every seed, so I am certain there is a new world within your world. *Whatever God calls for, He provides for.*

Additional Products, Materials and Programs

A wide range of resources are available for your personal development and growth, and for the improvement of small groups, families, leaders, businesses and communities. They include:

New Book Release

Single, Married, Separated and Life After Divorce

This book addresses the pressing issues of living, including resources for an effective single life. Topics discussed include: the foundational principles of a strong marriage, the silent issue of being separated—married but not living together, and the traumatic experience of life after divorce. This book is fast becoming a text book for youth groups, marriage seminars, singles ministries and counselor training. Myles Munroe used his unique style of simplicity and profound truth to produce another best-seller.

Audio and Video Tapes

Understanding Potential (Series)
Understanding God, Man, Male and Female (Series)
The Power of Purpose (Live at Azusa 90 and 91)
The Purpose of the Church (Series)
Principles of the Kingdom (Series)
The Purpose for the Male Man (Series)
The Purpose for the Female (Series)
(Video Tapes—$25 + postage; Audio Tapes—$5.00 + postage)

To order these fine books and tapes or to receive a catalog with a full listing of resources, write to:

Faithlife Resource Library
P. O. Box N9583
Nassau, Bahamas